THERE GOES THE BRIDE

THERE GOES THE BRIDE

by Ray Cooney and John Chapman

JOSEF WEINBERGER PLAYS

LONDON

First published in the United Kingdom in 1975
by Josef Weinberger Ltd
(pka English Theatre Guild Ltd/Warner Chappell Plays Ltd)
12-14 Mortimer Street, London, W1T 3JJ

Weinberger Classics edition first published 1990, reprinted 1995, 2001

ISBN 0 85676 202 4

Printed by Commercial Colour Press Plc, London E7

THERE GOES THE BRIDE was first presented by Ray Cooney Productions at the Palace Theatre, Westcliff on Sea, on 19 June, 1973 under the title of "Come Back To My Place", with the following cast:

Ursula Westerby	Elseph Gray
Judy Westerby	Susan Holderness
Dr. Gerald Drimmond	Geoffrey Sumner
Bill Shorter	Maurice Kaufmann
Timothy Westerby	Ray Cooney
Virginia Jones	Trudi Van Doorn
Daphne	Nan Munroe
Charles Babcock	Tom Chatto

Directed by John Chapman

The play was presented at The Criterion Theatre on 7 October, 1974, with the following cast:

Ursula Westerby	Jane Downs
Judy Westerby	Marguerite Hardiman
Dr. Gerald Drimmond	Geoffrey Sumner
Timothy Westerby	Bernard Cribbins
Bill Shorter	Terance Alexander
Daphne Drimmond	Peggy Mount
Polly Perkins	Trudi Van Doorn
Charles Babcock	Bill Pertwee

Directed by Jan Butlin

Designed by Hutchinson Scott.

PRESS APPRECIATIONS

"A wide-eyed wide-mouthed ghost from the Twenties had the audience gurgling with delight." *Sunday Times*

"I found myself surrendering to the ceaseless bombardment of familiar nonsense—laughing outright." *Daily Mail*

"Mr. Cooney and Mr. Chapman certainly know their jobs."
Evening Standard

"London's West End turns ever more hopefully to farce and comedy. Last night, unless I am mistaken, their quest struck gold. Echoing to the agitations of Peggy Mount and Bernard Cribbins, the Criterion welcomed a new farce by Ray Cooney and John Chapman which should be around for a year or two." *Daily Express*

"This farcial comedy is in full cry in the West End, it is unusually diverting because of its touch of fantasy . . . The situation ingeniously created by the authors, Ray Cooney and John Chapman, is exploited to the hilt by an excellent cast." *Evening News*

"There Goes The Bride" at the Criterion Theatre is a fiendishly clever farce that gets madder and funnier as it goes along . . . written by Ray Cooney and John Chapman, it has pace precision and wit." *Daily Mirror*

"The kinship of lunacy with farce is also explored adroitly by Ray Cooney and John Chapman in their latest production "There Goes The Bride."
Sunday Telegraph

"The spirit of true farce takes over." *The Times*

"I know people cry at Weddings but it's not often I weep over one in the theatre. And last night tears of joy coursed down my careworn face (seasoned in the search for a really good comedy). There were times when I thought the management would drag me out from "There Goes The Bride" to finish my howls of joy outside but all the audience were doing the same. To say this play goes as merrily as a marriage bell is like saying Ray Cooney and John Chapman are fairly funny writers whereas we know they are the only writers who have given us the funniest farces like "Dry Rot", "One for the Pot" and "Move Over Mrs. Markham". It's a zingy production so when you see it take three hankies, one to dry your eyes, one to stuff into your mouth and one to dry your tie."
Nottingham Evening Post

ACT ONE

The action takes place in the first floor lounge of a house in Kensington, furnished in a modern way but with elegance and taste.

Most of the R. wall of the set is taken up with two pairs of tall casement windows. There is a door D.R. leading into the study. U.C. are double doors leading into the hall, and D.L. a door leading to the dining room.

Visible through the open windows is the top of a red and white striped marquee.

TIME: *The present. 11 a.m. on a morning in summer.*

THE CURTAIN rises on an empty stage.

After a moment's pause, we hear:

URSULA (*off*) I do wish people wouldn't move things.

JUDY (*off*) Oh, Mother!

URSULA WESTERBY *enters wearing a house-coat. She is in her forties, and attractive.* JUDY, *who follows her onstage carrying her wedding-gown, is about twenty and not particularly glamorous. Her hair is still in rollers, and she is wearing a full-length slip complimentary to the wedding-gown.*

URSULA Who's taken the wretched work basket. (*She looks around.*)

JUDY Probably Grannie. Calm down, the cars won't be here for ages yet.

URSULA Honestly, this has been the worst morning of my life.

JUDY It's only a bit of stitching at the back of the dress.

URSULA Not that. It's what you told me in the bedroom that's really upset me.

JUDY You mean that Nicholas and I have been to bed together.

URSULA Yes!

JUDY Well, why did you ask?

URSULA Because I thought you'd say you hadn't.

JUDY What does it matter?

URSULA There won't be much mystery tonight.

JUDY Never mind, I'd rather have a good thriller than a mystery any time.

URSULA Go and look in the dining room. (*Still searching room for work basket.*)

(JUDY *exits.*)

And Whatever you do, don't disillusion your father. As far as he's concerned, you're still his little girl.

JUDY (*off*) Poor old Pop!

URSULA If he thought you weren't still a – well, that you and Nicholas had – well, I think he'd have a seizure. He can only just cope with his business worries, his weight and his heart murmurs. Is it there?

JUDY (*off*) 'Fraid not.

(JUDY *re–enters.*)

You can't tell me you and Daddy hadn't indulged in some heavy necking before you married.

URSULA Yes, but no more than that. It might be in the study. Your father had very definite views about sex. (*Opens door.*) He said it was like riding a bicycle. (*Exits into study.*)

JUDY (*examining her dress*) No wonder you've had problems.

URSULA (*off*) Got it. (*She re-enters with sewing basket.*)

JUDY Go on, what did he mean?

URSULA I forget now. (*Closes door.*) I think it was something to do with not trying to ride before you've bought your bike.

JUDY You tell him that Nicholas and I have had some practice, so he won't fall off tonight.

URSULA Come on, let's put your dress on. Is he back yet, d'you know?

(URSULA *helps* JUDY *into the wedding dress.*)

JUDY Daddy? No, I haven't seen him.

URSULA He went to get those bouquets ages ago. It's only just round the corner.

JUDY Don't flap.

URSULA Typical of your father. Leave everything to me, he said I'll get my secretary to order them all. Have some delivered here and some to the bridesmaids.

JUDY He just forgot.

URSULA If I hadn't brought it up at breakfast we'd have been pillaging all those little pots on the graves.

JUDY He's been working flat out. The advertising business is enough to drive anyone crazy.

URSULA He's so absentminded lately, it wouldn't surprise me if he'd gone to the office instead of the florist.

JUDY I don't know. A Church wedding, a choir, four hundred guests, a huge marquee in the garden, Savoy Hotel doing the catering. Honestly, Nicholas and I would've settled for a Registry Office.

URSULA (*threading a needle*) If your father knew what the pair of you had been up to he'd have had you married at sea.

(DR GERALD DRIMMOND *wanders in from the hall in a shirt, waistcoat and trousers of a morning suit. He is having a problem with his collar and front stud. He is in his late sixties. There are still signs of his perfect bedside manner but he's now somewhat vague and a little deaf. Whenever anyone can remember they speak up when they address him.*)

GERALD Anyone got a free hand?

JUDY In a minute grandad.

GERALD No, No, it's this damn stud.

URSULA (*looks out from behind* JUDY, *sewing*) Can't you see we're busy?

GERALD Couldn't see you at all actually.

URSULA I'll deal with you in a minute. Honestly, you spend a fortune on a wedding dress and the hook and eye comes off in your hand.

GERALD Oh – well, it looks very pretty to me. You look an absolute picture, Judy.

JUDY Thank you.

GERALD Darn lucky feller, that Roger.

JUDY Nicholas.

GERALD That's right, yes. (*Eyeing her rollers.*) Don't know what the Vicar's going to say about your hairdo, though.

JUDY (*chuckling*) Grandad.

GERALD Lots of activity down there in the garden this morning.

URSULA It's the caterers from the Savoy.

GERALD Very smart. I thought they were guests. I've been giving them champagne.

URSULA Never mind. Timothy hasn't come back with the flowers yet, has he?

GERALD What flowers?

URSULA For the bridesmaids, and buttonholes for you men.

GERALD Oh I don't think I can cope with a buttonhole as well as a collar stud.

URSULA If Tim makes us late this morning –

JUDY He won't. Haven't you finished yet?

URSULA No, darling, keep still.

GERALD By the way, anyone seen Timothy this morning?

URSULA That's just what I asked *you*.

GERALD Did you? When?

URSULA Just now.

GERALD You sure.

URSULA Of course I'm sure.

GERALD I don't think you did.

URSULA I said "Has he come back with the flowers?"

GERALD Did you?

URSULA
JUDY } (*together*) Yes.

GERALD What did I reply?

URSULA Never mind.

GERALD How very rude of me. I wanted to ask him about these black socks.

URSULA What's wrong with them?

(GERALD *lifts his trouser bottoms up and reveals that he has no socks on.*)

But you're not wearing any.

GERALD — I know that. Daphne didn't pack any. Timothy said he'd pop out this morning and buy me a pair.

JUDY — You shouldn't have bothered Daddy this morning.

GERALD — I'll never forget the time I was best man at Fatty Barnsley's wedding. No, wait a minute, was that his name or where he lived.

URSULA — Father! Couldn't mother help you.

GERALD — No, I don't think she ever met him.

JUDY — With your collar.

DAPHNE — No. Daphne's in as big a pickle as I am. Trying to get into her armour.

JUDY — Did you sleep alright?

GERALD — Yes, thanks, I always sleep well in someone else's bed. Always did. (*Chuckles.*) Used to worry your Granny. She'll be glad to get back to Bournemouth, I expect a couple of nights away from home is just about her limit.

(URSULA *has just now finished sewing* JUDY'S *popper.*)

URSULA — There. (*To* JUDY.) Hurry up now darling and not too much lacquer on your hair.

JUDY — No.

URSULA — I'll be up later to help you with the veil.

JUDY — O.K.

URSULA — And if I were you I'd wipe off some of that mascara. It'll run when you cry.

JUDY — Oh Mummy, I'm not going to cry.

URSULA Course you will, darling, we're all going to cry.

GERALD Quite right. You've got to observe the rituals on these occasions. Cry at weddings, laugh at funerals. Have you got something borrowed, something blue?

JUDY Yes Mummy's lent me her wedding veil and I've got a blue hanky.

GERALD So you're all set for when Nigel takes you down the aisle.

JUDY Nicholas.

GERALD (*puzzled*) Never heard of that custom.

JUDY Oh, Grandad!

(JUDY *exits.*)

URSULA Come on, father, let's get you sorted out.

GERALD They put too much starch in these damn things.

URSULA (*trying collar round his neck*) You can't blame the laundry. You're putting on a bit of weight.

(*As* URSULA *takes his collar off again the phone rings.*)

URSULA Answer that will you.

(*As he does so,* URSULA *goes to sewing basket to get a pair of small scissors to widen the stud hole.*)

GERALD (*into phone*) Hello, there. . . Mrs Westerby, no I'm afraid he isn't, can I help?. . . No, that's right he won't be at the office today, his daughter's getting married.

URSULA Who is it?

GERALD (*to* URSULA) It's a business call for Timothy.

URSULA Ask them to ring him at the Agency tomorrow.

GERALD (*into phone*) Ring the Agency tomorrow, will you?

URSULA And his name.

GERALD (*into phone*) And his name's Timothy Westerby.

URSULA No – his name.

GERALD (*to* URSULA) Oh yes. (*Into phone.*) Who's speaking please... Ah. (*To* URSULA.) It's a Mr Barrington Perkins-Brass.

URSULA Who?

GERALD Well that's what he said...Barrington Per – I'd better check that hadn't I. (*Into phone.*) Could you repeat that, please? (*To* URSULA.) It's Mr Barrington of Perkins Bra's.

(URSULA *hands* GERALD *his collar and takes the phone.*)

URSULA Hello Mr Barrington, this is Mrs Westerby. I'll tell my husband you phoned...yes I know it's important. Tim's been working on the campaign day and night...Well surely it can wait till tomorrow...Yes time's money, I'm sure that's true but it's his daughter's wedding day and I honestly can't see that another twenty-four hours is going to make your bra firm go bust – er, er broke...Yes, fine, alright I'll get him to ring you somehow, but don't be surprised if you hear a Vicar droning away in the background. (*She replaces the receiver.*) Astonishing isn't it. Everything in the advertising world is a matter of life and death.

GERALD (*blandly*) Yes, well being a doctor I never had that problem. What are you going to do now that Judy's off your hands?

URSULA Retire.

GERALD Retire?

URSULA Yes, gracefully of course. I shall start with a few weeks in bed.

GERALD And what about Tim?

URSULA Tim?

GERALD You know, the fellow who gives you the housekeeping every week.

URSULA Judy's going won't make any difference to him. He's completely wrapped up in the business.

GERALD Damn shame.

URSULA It'll be at least a week before he realises that Judy's left, I'm in bed and he's having breakfast by himself.

DAPHNE (*off*) Gerald! Where are you?

URSULA He's in here Mother.

(DAPHNE DRIMMOND *enters. She is in her late sixties, forceful and very much in command of all her faculties. She is wearing a very frilly attractive housecoat and has beautifully coiffured hair under her frilly mob cap.*)

DAPHNE Oh, Gerald! What on earth are you doing?

URSULA We're just fixing his collar mother, it's alright.

DAPHNE (*to* GERALD) But you were supposed to be helping me.

GERALD What?

DAPHNE (*whispering tersely*) With my undergarment.

GERALD Your what?

DAPHNE My girdle.

GERALD (*to* URSULA, *chuckling*) Oh yes, if you hear a loud twang in Church it'll be a toss-up between my collar and her corset.

DAPHNE Gerald! (*To* URSULA.) Have you got a pin, Ursula? I need one for my spray.

URSULA Pin? We haven't even got the flowers yet.

DAPHNE Is Timothy not back yet?

URSULA He will be, don't fuss.

DAPHNE Really Ursula. Come on Gerald, hurry up with that stud, or we'll never get to St. Barnabas.

GERALD St. where?

DAPHNE The church.

(*Throughout the ensuing dialogue,* DAPHNE *and* URSULA *endeavour to fix* GERALD'S *collar on him.*)

GERALD Oh. About this collar...

DAPHNE Never mind a collar. You need a lead. (*To* URSULA.) I told you not to send that husband of yours out this morning. He'll make us late, I know he will.

URSULA No he won't. Lift your chin up, father.

DAPHNE I bet the Babcocks will be there on time and they're coming from Sydney.

GERALD Sydney? Who's he?

DAPHNE Bridegroom's parents from Australia. (*Then to* URSULA.) Have you spoken to them since they arrived?

URSULA Not yet. They weren't due in until very late last night. Tim booked them into Claridges.

DAPHNE Did he. Let's hope he made a better job of it than ordering the flowers.

GERALD Careful, that's my Adam's apple you're pushing through the hole.

URSULA Sorry.

DAPHNE Swallow, that'll shift it. (*Then to* URSULA.) You should've checked with Mrs Babcock.

URSULA What?

(URSULA *and* DAPHNE *put cigarettes and chocolates in dishes on the tables.*)

DAPHNE What she intended to wear. We don't want to clash.

URSULA It's very difficult to check with someone you don't know, who lives on the other side of the world.

DAPHNE I only hope it's not lilac, that's all.

URSULA Anyway, there've been far more important things, arranging the choir, the music, the reception and four hundred guests.

GERALD What you and Tim need is a holiday, to some romantic spot, sort of second honeymoon.

URSULA I think our romantic days are over.

GERALD Can't be.

URSULA We've been married over twenty years.

GERALD Your mother and I have been married over forty years, but we still –

DAPHNE (*quickly*) Gerald! (*Goes to help* GERALD *do up cuff links etc.*)

GERALD Beg pardon, dear. (*To* URSULA.) Anyway, that's what we did when you got married didn't we Daphne?

DAPHNE Yes, dear.

GERALD I got a locum in to look after the practice. Nice chap, Doctor er – Doctor something or other, moustache and bright ginger hair, or was that his wife?

DAPHNE Dr Saunders.

GERALD Very likely – Anyway you'd just married and your mother and I plumped for a second honeymoon. Two wonderful weeks in Monte Carlo, swimming, sailing and gambling – out of this world.

DAPHNE You're getting your holidays mixed. When Ursula got married we went on a cruise to the Canary Islands.

GERALD Did we?

DAPHNE Yes. I wasn't even with you on the Monte Carlo holiday. You went by yourself.

GERALD No wonder I enjoyed it so much.

DAPHNE Oooh!

(*The phone rings.*)

GERALD (*to* URSULA) Do you want me to answer that?

URSULA No. Take him away mother.

DAPHNE Put him away!

(DAPHNE *exits with* GERALD *as* URSULA *picks up the phone.*)

URSULA (*on phone*) 0343...No, he's not, could you ring him at the office tomorrow...Oh, I'm so sorry Mr Babcock. Welcome to London. How are you? Haven't we chosen a gorgeous day for it. I'm sure your Nicholas is just as nervous as our Judy. He's such a dear boy, we're so fond of him and he's told us all about you and Mrs Babcock. What was the plane journey like...Bloody what?...awful. Oh dear. Well if you will live in Australia.

(*Laughs, then suddenly.*) – nothing at all, I'm sure it's a lovely country, but you're here now and safely at Claridges. Oh, you're not at Claridges...but I thought Timothy had booked you in...Oh, I'm so terribly sorry. So where did you end up...Oh, well, some parts of Notting Hill Gate are very attractive...not where you are, no...

(TIMOTHY *enters looking agitated and slightly breathless. He is in his forties, and pleasant looking but slightly neurotic. He is dressed smartly but casually. Under one arm he carries a large box full of flowers and bouquets, and under the other he has a life size wood cut-out of a 1920 "flapper" girl but with no head.*)

TIMOTHY Hello, darling. Sorry I'm late. Listen I had to go to the office, I've had this thing made up. I've had the most fabulous idea.

URSULA Sh! It's Mr Babcock.

TIMOTHY Oh, heavens, I'll take it. Would you hold that...yes and that. Thank you, darling. (*Pushing the flowers and cut-out onto* URSULA *and takes the phone. On phone.*) Now I've gone right off the idea of the girl wearing no bra, and I'll tell you why.

URSULA (*trying to attract his attention*) Darling, it's not Mr Barrington.

TIMOTHY (*pressing on*) It's alright in the magazines but bare boobs on the telly can be very dicey, can't they?

URSULA It's Mr Babcock.

TIMOTHY My main concern here is the homage of your brassiere, and I've decided to go for the 1920's look.

URSULA Timothy, it's Mr Babcock!

TIMOTHY (*to* URSULA) I know. Managing Director from Perkins Bra's.

URSULA No, bridgeroom's father from Sydney, Australia.

TIMOTHY (*shattered*) Oh, my God. (*Then gaily into phone.*) Sorry about that, Bluey!

(URSULA *parks cut-out and flowers.*)

TIMOTHY (*into phone*) Now what can I do for you on this beautiful day Mr Babcock?...Flowers? They're at Claridges...You're not?...Well where are you?...The what hotel, where?...Where did that come about?...A right bloody cockup, yes. I'm most terribly sorry, you'll be thinking your son's father-in-law's a bit of an idiot. (*Chuckles.*)...Oh... Well, I'll put them in a taxi and have them sent to the Church. Good on you, Cobblers. (*Puts the phone down.*) I don't know, some people seem able to cope.

URSULA Never mind, darling, it's not that important.

TIMOTHY (*indicating the phone*) He'll never forgive us. Twelve thousand miles he's come for his son's Society Wedding and thanks to me he's holed up by the Goods Depot of Paddington Station.

URSULA Have a little drink, steady your nerves.

TIMOTHY Yes – no, better not, it's time for my pills. (*Takes a small bottle out of his pocket and removes a pill from it.*)

URSULA Which ones – the "pepper uppers" or the "calmer downers"?

TIMOTHY I think these are the "keeper downers".

URSULA Do try and relax, darling.

TIMOTHY Relax, with all this going on? Have you seen the garden? (*Calling out window.*) Oi, you! Yes, you. . .don't do that in the geraniums please. What? Oh, it's the gardener, finishing the watering. (*To* URSULA.) And do you know what that stupid catering manager's done now?

URSULA I don't know why you let him upset you so much.

TIMOTHY I specifically asked for that nice cheap Danish caviar at 30p. a pot – and what's he got down there? Two tons of the Russian stuff at five quid an ounce.

URSULA Father's right, we need a nice long holiday.

TIMOTHY (*taking his pill*) By the time I've finished paying for this wedding we'll be lucky if we can afford a day trip to Brighton.

URSULA We can manage a fortnight somewhere.

TIMOTHY Oh darling if I could find the time it would be lovely. (*Drinks glass of water.*)

URSULA That's just what we need, a second honeymoon. Wouldn't it be marvellous.

TIMOTHY Yes, it would, as long as I can remember what I did on the first one.

URSULA You need a break. Bill can manage without you for a bit.

TIMOTHY Yes, I have been getting a little – er – you know – lately.

URSULA You're not getting all neurotic about your health again.

TIMOTHY Not really, I think all the pills seem to be integrating quite nicely. No I'm fine. (*Getting cut-out.*) It's this Perkin's Bra campaign. It does mean a lot to the firm. Now tell me, what do you think of this? (*He holds up the cut-out.*)

URSULA You mean apart from the fact that it gives me an inferiority complex.

TIMOTHY Yes – no. (*Excitedly.*) I mean wouldn't this make you rush out and buy a Perkin's bra?

URSULA I don't know darling – Let's put it to the vote at St. Barnabas, shall we?

(BILL SHORTER *enters from the hall. He is handsome and rakish in his late forties. He is dressed in a beautifully cut morning suit, and is carrying opened champagne bottle and the remains of a caviar spread biscuit.*)

BILL Morning, Ursula my darling. God, the bride will have to steam some to look lovelier than you.

URSULA Thank you, Bill.

BILL (*to* TIM) Hi, partner.

TIMOTHY 'Morning.

BILL (*holding up bottle*) I picked this up from your catering feller downstairs. Couldn't you do better than that?

TIMOTHY I beg your pardon?

BILL Still, this cheap Danish caviar's not bad. You can hardly tell it from the real thing.

TIMOTHY That is the real thing. (BILL *pops the biscuit in his mouth.*) That's another five quid's worth gone in one gulp.

BILL Are you not bothering to change?

TIMOTHY I had to go to the office. It's been another one of those mornings.

BILL What mornings? (*Starts pouring two glasses of Champagne.*)

URSULA One of those mornings you'd know nothing about, Bill. How many of the clients have rung you at home today.

BILL None. If they ring me at home I just say I'm in the middle of seducing my secretary.

URSULA It wouldn't surprise me.

BILL They don't ring me at the flat after that I can tell you.

TIMOTHY They're not too keen to ring him at the office either.

URSULA It seems most unfair. You two are supposed to be equal partners.

BILL So we are, but I'm strictly an eleven till three man.

TIMOTHY And that's just his lunch hour.

URSULA (*to* BILL) You haven't had Perkin's Bra on this morning have you?

BILL No they don't carry my size. (*Crosses with glass to* URSULA.)

URSULA Well they think nothing of badgering my Timothy on his daughter's wedding day.

TIMOTHY Perkin's Bra's?

BILL (*handing her a glass of Champagne*) Come on old thing, don't get yourself in a state. Leave the nervous breakdowns to Timothy.

TIMOTHY (*to* URSULA) You didn't say Perkins had rung, did you?

URSULA Yes.

TIMOTHY Listen, Bill, we've got to come up with something for that campaign, otherwise we'll lose the account.

BILL Don't worry about it today.

TIMOTHY Now I've had what I think is a fabulous idea. Just take a look –

BILL (*interrupting*) Have a glass of bubbly.

TIMOTHY — No, I can't because it doesn't go with the pills.

BILL — Please yourself. (*Raises the glass to* URSULA.) Cheers.

URSULA — Cheers.

TIMOTHY — I think the way to sell Perkin's Bra is, –

(*They drink as* GERALD *pops his head in the door.*)

GERALD — Ursula, you got such a thing as a pair of pliers?

URSULA — We don't want any handiwork done this morning, thank you.

GERALD — No it's your mother's corset. We still can't get her into the damn thing.

URSULA — Alright, I'll deal with her when I've done Judy. (*As she goes.*) Bill see that Tim gets changed, will you?

GERALD — (*seeing* TIMOTHY *with cut-out*) You make a lovely couple, don't you?

(URSULA *bustles* GERALD *out and exits.*)

TIMOTHY — You see the beauty of the 1920's girl is that's when the bra was first introduced. I know I'm on to something, Bill. Can't you picture the Perkins girl with the funny hat, the cupid's bow mouth, feather boa, frilly skirt, beads, the lot.

BILL — I suppose a 1920 flapper might be an idea.

TIMOTHY — (*excitedly*) Did you say flapper?

BILL — Yes.

TIMOTHY — Well, that's it, Flapper! "Perkins Takes the Flop out of Flappers". I'll ring them right away. (*Goes to phone.*)

BILL — Ring who?

TIMOTHY Perkins.

BILL Don't be silly. You've got to be dressed. In half an hour you and the bride are leaving for St. Barnabas.

TIMOTHY Well if I get dressed quickly, perhaps we could call in at Perkins' offices on the way. My Perkins Flapper. It's terriffic.

BILL The Perkins' offices are in Regent Street.

TIMOTHY It's only a little detour.

BILL Detour?

TIMOTHY And we'll have a driver so parking won't be a problem. (*Suddenly.*) Socks!

BILL I beg your pardon.

TIMOTHY I've just remembered I was supposed to buy Gerald a pair of socks on my way to the florists.

BILL That's not important.

TIMOTHY Oh, and the flowers!

BILL They're here, relax.

TIMOTHY No, they're ours, I've got to get some round to Mr and Mrs Babcock at Claridges.

BILL Calm down.

TIMOTHY No, wait. They're not at Claridges. I'd forgotten to book them in.

BILL Well where are they staying?

TIMOTHY I've forgotten that as well. I'll ring Claridges and ask them – no – I'll ring Perkins first and speak to that Mr er – oh what's his name, Compton, Bradman.

BILL Barrington.

TIMOTHY That's him. And tell him I'll pick him up from Regent Street.

BILL Pick him up?

TIMOTHY Yes, then in the car on the way to the church I can explain to him about Perkins taking the flop out of flappers.

BILL (*trying to calm him down*) Timothy –

TIMOTHY (*excitedly*) It's a fantastic idea Bill. I wouldn't be surprised if she didn't turn out to be bigger than the Bisto Kids. I can see her now in all the magazines, on all the hoardings, up and down escalators, and if we get her on television, we could actually have her singing and dancing. (*Sings.*) "Won't You Perkins With Me –" "Fits your B-U-S-T".

BILL Oh, now, Tim –

(TIMOTHY *continues to sing and dance the Charleston. As he gets near the door,* GERALD *enters and* TIMOTHY *gets knocked on the head by the door. He totters with a dazed expression on his face and collapses behind the settee.* GERALD *doesn't see what he's done, rubs his hand.*)

GERALD Ah Mr Shorter, any news of my socks. (*He sees* TIMOTHY.) Who's that?

BILL It's Timothy. I think the excitement's been to much for him. (*To* TIMOTHY.) You alright, old man?

TIMOTHY (*weakly*) I'm lovely.

BILL He's lovely.

GERALD Head between the knees, that helps.

BILL Look here, get some cold flannels.

GERALD Flannels, yes. (*Looking down at his trousers.*) Grey or White?

BILL Either, it doesn't matter.

GERALD — You won't forget to ask him about my socks, will you?

BILL — No.

(GERALD *exits.* BILL *shuts the door.*)

Come on Tim, Up you get. Pills or no pills I'll get you a brandy. How are you feeling.

(*He goes to the drinks table and pours a brandy. His back is to the sofa.*)

TIMOTHY — I'm alright.

(TIMOTHY *rises. Simultaneously "Polly Perkins" rises with him from behind the sofa. [*N.B. *The actress playing* POLLY *has been hidden behind the sofa from the beginning of the play.]* POLLY *is about 22 and dressed as the complete flapper of the 1920's including short hair and make-up. She is completely extrovert, very kooky and madly attractive. During* BILL'S *ensuing speech,* TIMOTHY *happens to see* POLLY *standing beside him and tries to work out who she is and how she got there, while* POLLY *gives him a dazzling smile.*)

BILL — Oh, good, I fully expected to be given the job of looking after the bride and probably the bride's mother, and possibly even the bridegroom, but I was hoping the father of the bride would be able to stand on his own two feet. I suggest you stop worrying about Gerald's socks, Babcock's flowers and Perkin's Bra's, and just you concentrate on getting yourself ready for the church.

(*By now* TIMOTHY *has walked over to* BILL. BILL *gives him the drink.*)

There we are.

TIMOTHY — (*takes glass*) No thank you. Bill how long has she been there?

BILL — Huh?

TIMOTHY The – er – the young lady.

BILL Young lady?

TIMOTHY (*starting to get worried*) Yes. The one with the frilly skirt, the feather boa – and the little hat – er – you know, the girl.

BILL What girl?

(*For the next few seconds, although no expression crosses* TIMOTHY'S *face, his mind is in a whirl as he tries to fathom out the implications of* BILL'S *reply. Finally he knocks back his brandy.*)

TIMOTHY I beg your pardon?

BILL I said what girl.

TIMOTHY Yes. Yes, that's what I thought you said. What do you mean what girl?

BILL Just what I say, what girl.

TIMOTHY The girl over there with the funny hat and the beads and the frilly – my Perkins flapper.

BILL Perkins Flapper?

(TIMOTHY *looks at* POLLY, *who smiles, then back to* BILL.)

TIMOTHY (*thinking* BILL'S *joking*) Come off it Bill – stop being funny.

BILL Me?

(TIMOTHY *looks at* POLLY *and tentatively feels her arm and is reassured to find that it's solid.*)

TIMOTHY (*chuckling*) Now stop messing about?

BILL What did you do that for?

TIMOTHY Do what for?

BILL You just went – (*He mimes squeezing thin air.*)

TIMOTHY (*still chuckling*) Yes of course I did. (*He squeezes her arm.*)

BILL You're doing it again.

TIMOTHY (*still chuckling*) I know I am.

BILL Are you pulling my leg?

TIMOTHY (*wiping the smile off*) No, squeezing her arm.

BILL Look Tim, cut the gags, there's not a lot of time.

TIMOTHY Very funny Bill, but just explain how you sneaked the young lady in.

BILL Never take a joke too far.

TIMOTHY That's enough Bill. (*To* POLLY.) Please excuse my friend.

BILL Look, it's a little tap on a head you've had.

TIMOTHY (*to* POLLY) I'm sorry.

BILL And so am I! You're beginning to worry me Timothy.

(*During the next part of* BILL'*s speech,* POLLY *comes up to him and saucily does the Charleston around him.*)

I mean if you're not joking it's very disturbing. So admit that you've been kidding and we'll say no more about it.

TIMOTHY (*to* POLLY) Will you stop that.

BILL No, I won't.

TIMOTHY I was talking to her.

BILL Now look, any more of this and I'll get Ursula in here.

TIMOTHY (*agitatedly*) No please.

BILL Well pull yourself together.

TIMOTHY (*to* POLLY) Will you please stop bouncing up and down.

BILL I'm not bouncing up and down!

TIMOTHY Not you! (*Opens study doors.*) Would you mind waiting in here for a moment.

BILL Yes I would! I'm warning you Timothy, I'll get Ursula.

TIMOTHY You can see her, of course you can see her!

BILL I can't.

TIMOTHY She's dancing all around you.

BILL What's she doing the Charleston!?

TIMOTHY You *can* see her.

BILL That does it!

(*He storms out into the hall.*)

POLLY What a simply spiffing lark.

TIMOTHY It's another one of his damn silly jokes, isn't it. I suppose you and he have dreamt this up between you.

POLLY No.

TIMOTHY Well where have you come from?

POLLY (*gaily*) Don't know.

TIMOTHY You're not from Market Research are you?

POLLY What's that?

TIMOTHY Now come on, somebody must have sent you here to be my Perkins Flapper.

POLLY Perkins Flapper?

TIMOTHY Why are you all dressed up like that?

POLLY Don't know.

(She starts to sing and dance "The Black Bottom".)

TIMOTHY Thank you Miss Perkins, very nice. Would you get in touch with our Agency next week.

(She continues to sing and dance.)

Would you stop that. I don't know what you think you're up to –

POLLY Ooh, I love that stern look.

TIMOTHY Or who sent you here.

POLLY Neither do I. Isn't it simply spiffing.

TIMOTHY No it's not. You've chosen a very busy morning Miss Perkins. I mean Miss – er – what is your name?

POLLY Golly, I don't know.

TIMOTHY You don't know.

POLLY No. What's yours?

TIMOTHY That's neither here nor there.

POLLY No, don't tell me, let me guess. George.

TIMOTHY George?

POLLY No. Jack? Ralph?

TIMOTHY Timothy.

POLLY Oh I adore that.

TIMOTHY It's quite ordinary really.

POLLY It's beautiful.

TIMOTHY Timothy Westerby.

POLLY *(ecstatically)* Oh!

TIMOTHY *(playing it down)* I can't take a lot of credit for it –

POLLY *(savouring it)* Timothy Westerby.

TIMOTHY Actually I have a middle name as well.

POLLY I bet it's not as super as Timothy.

TIMOTHY No it's not. It's Royston.

POLLY (*excitedly*) Oh delicious! Timothy Royston Westerby. How do you do, Timothy.

TIMOTHY (*dumbly shaking hands*) How do you do, Miss Perkins.

(GERALD *enters with a pair of trousers. He walks straight up to* POLLY *who of course he can't see and speaks to* TIMOTHY *who is standing the other side of her*.)

GERALD Hello old feller, I've got your flannels, I could only find white. You got my socks?

(*For a few seconds* TIMOTHY *tries to take in the confirmation of the fact that* POLLY *can be seen only by himself*.)

GERALD (*louder*) I said have you got my socks?

POLLY Hey, he can't see me.

GERALD (*after a pause*) Well have you, old man?

POLLY 'Fraid not old fruit. (*To* TIMOTHY.) He can't hear me either.

GERALD (*yelling*) Well have you?

TIMOTHY (*weakly*) No.

GERALD Oh. Well I still need a pair of black socks.

TIMOTHY Yes, you do. (*Peering round* POLLY*'s right shoulder*.)

GERALD And you definitely didn't get 'em?

TIMOTHY No. I got something else instead.

GERALD Dark blue?

TIMOTHY I-I-I didn't get socks at all, actually.

(*Peers round* POLLY*'s left shoulder*.)

GERALD You got a stiff neck or something.

POLLY This is spiffing fun.

TIMOTHY No, it's terrible.

GERALD Oh, I'm sorry. You've been sitting in a draught I expect.

(TIMOTHY *hastily pulls* GERALD *to one side.*)

TIMOTHY Gerald. . .(*As he passes* POLLY.) Excuse me.

GERALD (*thinking* TIM *was addressing him*) Yes, certainly.

TIMOTHY What's it called when a chap keeps seeing a girl that nobody else knows about?

GERALD Adultery.

TIMOTHY No. I mean suppose he keeps talking to someone who apparently isn't there. What's that?

GERALD Insanity.

TIMOTHY (*laughs nervously*) Insanity! (*Rips trousers in two, then points towards* POLLY.) Gerald, what can you see over there?

GERALD The chair you mean?

TIMOTHY No! Just in front of the chair.

(POLLY *gives him a cheery wave.*)

Can't you see anything? You know, waving?

GERALD Has this got anything to do with my socks?

TIMOTHY Oh Lord! (*To* POLLY.) I'm not going to let you spoil my daughter's wedding day.

GERALD Damnit, all I want is a pair of socks.

TIMOTHY In a minute!

(TIMOTHY *then marches to study door, opens it and gesticulates for* POLLY *to go in. She eventually does so, and he closes the door.*)

GERALD That was an extraordinary thing to do.

TIMOTHY Hmm?

GERALD I've never seen a fella do a thing like that before.

TIMOTHY Like what?

GERALD Well, I don't know whether I can. Um...

(GERALD *mimes the arm actions that he saw* TIMOTHY *do.*)

TIMOTHY (*trying to brazen it out*) Yes, that's right, I did.

GERALD What is it? Semaphore?

TIMOTHY No, I opened the door – to let some fresh air in. (*He starts to lead* GERALD *towards the hall.*)

GERALD Oh, fresh air. (*Pausing en route.*) And what was all this about? (*Waving his arm again.*)

TIMOTHY Oh, well, that was circulating it.

(*Apparently satisfied,* GERALD *moves towards hall again.*)

GERALD Oh was that what it was.

(TIMOTHY *closes double doors behind* GERALD, *rushes to the study door, opens it and beckons* POLLY *out.*)

TIMOTHY Now come out of there, Miss Perkins, or whatever your damn silly name is.

(POLLY *dances out, grabs* TIMOTHY'*s arm and dances him round, singing "Tea for Two".*)

(*Protesting.*) No, no, stop that, I have a wedding to go to...please, Miss –

(*The double doors open and* DAPHNE *enters.*)

(*Seeing her.*) Oh, my God!

(He quickly dances POLLY *to the study door, propels her through and quickly shuts the door. He continues dancing, but turning to see* DAPHNE'*s thunderous face, tries to escape by the window.)*

DAPHNE Timothy! Come back. What on earth are you doing?

TIMOTHY *(returning)* Loosening up this new pair of trousers. Tell me, did you see anything when you came in just now?

DAPHNE Yes, I most certainly did!

TIMOTHY Oh, thank goodness. I thought Bill was playing one of his damn silly jokes, and he's got Gerald in on it, too. What did you see?

DAPHNE Just you being stupid as usual. *(She imitates* TIM'*s dance steps.)*

TIMOTHY Only...? Oh my God...*(Turning away.)*

DAPHNE Timothy, you are not even dressed yet.

TIMOTHY *(nervously)* No. I had to get the flappers from the florist.

DAPHNE The what?

TIMOTHY I mean the flowers. *(Getting box of flowers.)*

DAPHNE Oh, good. Have you got my spray there?

TIMOTHY Yes – er – take your pick.

DAPHNE *(choosing one)* That's nice.

TIMOTHY *(taking it back)* Yes, that's the bride's.

(DAPHNE *picks up another one.)*

(Taking it from her.) That's the mother of the bride's. Yours is up this end of the box, with the other guests.

DAPHNE Guests. *(Coolly.)* Thank you. *(She picks out a small rose, which promptly droops in her hand.)*

TIMOTHY I'm sorry Daphne, but it's the best they could do at such short notice. (*Looking at the drooping flower.*) Do what Percy Thrower says – talk to it.

DAPHNE I'll talk to you in a minute.

TIMOTHY (*thrusting the box at her*) Would you be good enough to dish the rest of them out?

DAPHNE I came in for the work basket.

TIMOTHY (*gives it to her*) What a good idea, work basket, yes. It'll give you something to do, because these wedding services can drag on a bit, can't they? (DAPHNE *moves towards the hall, and* TIMOTHY *follows. Lifting up head of rose again.*) And don't worry about that. It'll be alright when it's had a drink.

DAPHNE (*darkly*) A double brandy, at least.

(*She exits and* TIMOTHY *closes the doors behind her.*)

TIMOTHY Yes, well...see you later, then,

(TIMOTHY *crosses swiftly to the study door, opens it and gestures to* POLLY *to come out. Whilst he is doing this,* GERALD *enters from the hall, concealing a pair of golfing socks, each one rolled up tightly in his hand. Noticing* GERALD, TIMOTHY *flaps his cardigan in doorway.*)

GERALD Still circulating it?

TIMOTHY (*immediately closing the door*) Yes, I've got to keep it moving, otherwise it settles in the corners.

GERALD By the way, I was wrong. Daphne did pack a pair of socks. (*Letting the socks unroll from his hands to the bottom of his trousers.*) What do you think of these?

TIMOTHY No I don't think so. Not with the morning suit, Gerald.

GERALD Perhaps you're right.

(URSULA *and* BILL *enter from the hall.* URSULA *has changed into her dress.*)

URSULA Timothy, do you realise that the cars will be here in half an hour?

TIMOTHY (*agitatedly*) Yes, don't worry. I'll be ready. How's our – our – how's. . . ?

URSULA Judy?

TIMOTHY Yes, that's the one. How is she?

URSULA She's alright. How are you?

TIMOTHY (*with* POLLY'*s gesture*) Oh, I'm spiffing, spiffing.

URSULA Spiffing?

TIMOTHY I mean fine.

URSULA Are you sure dear? Bill says you've been behaving very strangely.

TIMOTHY That's nonsense.

BILL Come off it, you were jabbering away to yourself, opening and shutting doors.

TIMOTHY I was doing no such thing.

BILL I promise you Ursula, he was – (*He mimes what* TIMOTHY *did at the door.*)

GERALD God, there's another one at it. (*To* URSULA.) What are these two, a couple of tic-tac men?

BILL You've caught him at it as well, have you?

GERALD Yes, just now, by the study door.

BILL I told you. (*Goes to study door.*) He marched straight over to the study door, opened it, and said –

(*He opens it and* POLLY *walks in gaily.*)

TIMOTHY Get out!

GERALD (*putting a hand to his ear*) My God.

URSULA Darling there's no need to shout,

TIMOTHY I wasn't shouting, I just said get out,

URSULA But you said it to Bill.

TIMOTHY (*madly thinking*) Did I? Yes, well, quite right. He's always coming into my house, opening and shutting all my doors, and I won't have it.

URSULA Timothy!

TIMOTHY And I want him to get out.

BILL Charming.

URSULA But he's our oldest friend.

TIMOTHY Yes and I'm fed up with him. Twenty years he's been wandering in and out of here, pinching my whisky and your bottom.

URSULA } (*together*) Timothy!
BILL } Damn cheek.

TIMOTHY Don't you deny it.

POLLY Oh I love that stern look.

TIMOTHY (*smiles at her*) Do you really? (*Then immediately to the others.*) I didn't say anything?

(*The others all look at him warily.*)

BILL I think perhaps we ought to put him to bed.

URSULA On the morning of Judy's wedding?

BILL Just a quick lay down.

POLLY That sounds fun.

TIMOTHY No it doesn't. (*Hastily to the others.*) I mean, no we can't.

URSULA We?

TIMOTHY Yes, we. You and I darling. We can't lie down. It's our daughter's honeymoon, it's not ours.

URSULA (*placating him*) Timothy, darling.

TIMOTHY What on earth would Judy say? She'd think we were a shocking pair.

GERALD Any pair will do, as long as they're dark.

URSULA (*pushing him to the door*) Father, please, go and look through Timothy's drawers.

GERALD It was socks I wanted really.

(*He exits.*)

TIMOTHY (*businesslike*) Right. Now if you've all stopped messing about, I'm going up to get changed.

POLLY (*following him*) I'll come and help you.

TIMOTHY (*stops*) No. (*To the others.*) Nobody's to help me. I don't want any help.

BILL Alright, alright.

TIMOTHY I don't need any help. I'm going up there, by myself. (*To* POLLY.) And you're not to follow me. (*Quickly to* BILL.) And you're not to follow me. I'll come back when I'm dressed.

POLLY I'll be waiting.

TIMOTHY Very well. (*He moves towards hall.*)

(*She casually goes into her own version of "My Blue Heaven" singing and dancing around* URSULA.)

POLLY (*singing*) Just Timmy and Me and Wifey makes three we're happy in my blue heaven –

(TIMOTHY *hesitates apprehensively at the door, then comes back to* URSULA *again.*)

TIMOTHY (*hissing at* POLLY) Stop that!

URSULA Well, go on, then.

TIMOTHY Yes. Yes, I will.

(*Worried about* POLLY'*s dancing, he tries to attract* POLLY'*s attention by indicating to her with jerks of the head and gesticulations that she should go into the study, but she refuses, and smiles coyly.* URSULA *and* BILL *try to humour* TIMOTHY *and participate in the waving gestures, until* TIMOTHY *goes into a 'shaping up' stance to* BILL.)

BILL God, he's off again.

TIMOTHY On second thoughts I'll get changed down here.

URSULA In the drawing room?

TIMOTHY Yes, it's safer. And I don't want you two to watch.

BILL I think he's cracking up.

URSULA He wouldn't dare.

TIMOTHY (*to* URSULA) Just fetch my clothes and then stay out.

URSULA There's no need to speak to me like that. You've chosen a fine day to start being masterful.

TIMOTHY You don't like my stern look, do you?

POLLY (*in his ear*) I do.

TIMOTHY Yes, I know you do. (*To* URSULA.) But you don't.

BILL He's flipped.

TIMOTHY I've what?

BILL He hasn't been the same since he had that tap on the head.

URSULA Tap on the head? (*To* TIM.) Darling, you never told me.

TIMOTHY (*to* URSULA) Just fetch my clothes!

URSULA Alright!

TIMOTHY And take the phantom bottom pincher of Putney with you.

URSULA (*quickly*) Come on Bill.

(BILL *and* URSULA *exit into the hall.*)

TIMOTHY (*rounding on* POLLY) Will you please go.

(BILL *pops his head back in.*)

BILL (*shouting*) We are going.

(*He goes again.*)

TIMOTHY (*quietly*) Will you please go.

POLLY Where to?

TIMOTHY Wherever it was you came from.

POLLY Where's that?

TIMOTHY I don't know! You've got me at it now. the point is you can't stay here. I've got to get to the Church for my daughter's wedding in forty-five minutes.

POLLY Sounds gorgeous. I'll come with you.

TIMOTHY That's not a good idea.

POLLY Ooh, they're grey aren't they?

TIMOTHY I beg your pardon?

POLLY Your eyes. I thought they were blue.

TIMOTHY They are blue.

POLLY No they're not, they change colour in different lights.

TIMOTHY Do they really?

POLLY (*suddenly*) Hey, what colour are mine?

TIMOTHY I don't know.

POLLY Well do have a look, please.

(*He peers at her closely.*)

TIMOTHY Well that one's brown. And that one's brown. They're both brown.

POLLY (*lovingly*) Isn't it absolutely ripping finding out about one another.

TIMOTHY Under different circumstances, yes I suppose it could be, but not today, thank you very much.

(POLLY *moves still closer.*)

POLLY Oh I'm all wobbly being this close to you. You sure you're not getting this feeling?

TIMOTHY No, I'm afraid not and I do have Judy's wedding and the reception, and as father of the bride, I have to make a speech.

(*He takes a sheet of paper out of his inside pocket.*)

I haven't even finished yet, and I'm not very good at them at the best of times. So run along now please Miss Perkins and – and – and –

(POLLY *now gives him a kiss which she starts calmly and then gradually increases the passion. When she finally breaks,* TIMOTHY'*s face is a picture of dazed happiness. He tears his speech in half and tosses it over his shoulder.*)

TIMOTHY Fantastic!

(BILL *re-enters carrying* TIMOTHY'*s morning suit.*)

BILL Now here you are, and for God's sake get a move on.

TIMOTHY (*dreamily thinking of his kiss*) Fantastic.

BILL (*looking at the suit*) If you've seen one you've seen 'em all.

TIMOTHY Oh, what a kisser.

BILL (*apprehensively feels his face*) What?

TIMOTHY Fabulous.

BILL (*patting* TIMOTHY *on the cheek*) Come on old man. Easy does it.

TIMOTHY (*coming to*) Oh, hello Bill.

BILL Are you alright?

TIMOTHY Fine, fantastic, absolutely fantastic.

BILL Good, that is a relief.

TIMOTHY (*turns to* POLLY) And so is Miss Perkins.

BILL Oh, for God's sake! You're not starting all that again.

TIMOTHY Standing right there. (*To* POLLY.) Aren't you?

(POLLY *nods.*)

TIMOTHY There you are. What did I tell you.

BILL I didn't hear anything.

TIMOTHY Of course you didn't, she only nodded.

(POLLY *kisses his ear, and makes him giggle.*)

BILL Look, Tim, if you carry on like this they're going to cart you off.

TIMOTHY (*to* POLLY) Oh, I've got that feeling now.

BILL Feeling, What feeling?

TIMOTHY Bill listen –

BILL Now you just listen to me and tell Polly Perkins to pin her ears back too.

POLLY Oh I like that.

BILL (*pressing on*) D'you realise that you've totally disrupted the entire morning of your daughter's wedding...

TIMOTHY (*to* BILL) Hang on, Miss Perkins was speaking.

BILL (*sarcastically*) Oh, I'm sorry.

POLLY I like that.

TIMOTHY What do you like?

POLLY That name, Polly.

TIMOTHY (*to* BILL) Do you hear that?

BILL No.

TIMOTHY She likes it.

BILL What?

TIMOTHY Polly.

BILL Oh, good. Now listen, you've already upset Ursula by shouting at her so please, please get dressed before you do any more damage.

TIMOTHY Bill, I don't know how to explain this to you but the most extraordinary thing has happened to me. I know the fact that you and the others can't see her and I can does seem a bit unlikely –

BILL A bit!

TIMOTHY But there are more things in heaven and earth Horatio.

BILL (*looking around*) Horatio?

TIMOTHY I mean I thought she was in my imagination until just now when she kissed me.

BILL Oh, you have made progress.

(DAPHNE *enters behind them. She is now dressed and looking angry.*)

TIMOTHY I tell you Bill I've had a few kisses in my time, but I can honestly say that one just now practically took my head off.

(DAPHNE *reacts to this thinking that* TIMOTHY *is addressing* BILL.)

I tell you Bill, I'm still wobbling.

DAPHNE Timothy!

POLLY Oooh, look, that hat's a hoot!

(TIMOTHY *and* BILL *jump.* TIMOTHY *grabs* POLLY *and pushes her into the dining room.*)

TIMOTHY (*turns round*) Oh, Daphne, you're dressed. You managed to get into the thing. . . (*Corset mime.*)

DAPHNE (*outraged*) What thing?

TIMOTHY (*changing course*) The hat. Looks very nice up there. Bill and I were just having. . .

DAPHNE I'd rather not know what you and Bill were just having. I don't know if you two have been drinking or what, but you'd better go straight upstairs and comfort Ursula.

BILL Good idea.

DAPHNE And while you're at it, kindly inform the Savoy catering manager that I'm not Mrs Smollett, who's late; I have not forgotten my uniform; and I'm not here to stack and wipe.

(*The telephone rings.* TIMOTHY *answers it.*)

TIMOTHY Hello. . .Oh, it's you, Mr Babcock. Everything going smoothly your end? (*Laughs.*) Jolly good, jolly good.

BILL What's he say?

TIMOTHY (*hand over mouthpiece*) He says where the hell are the bloody flowers. (*Into phone.*) I was just about to send you some when Polly arrived.

BILL (*snatching phone*) Hello, Mr Babcock, it's Bill Shorter here, Tim's partner . . . . . .
Polly? . . . . . . Did he? Oh, yes, Polly's the new kitten.

DAPHNE (*looking round*) Kitten?

BILL It's a wedding present from Doctor and Mrs Drimmond.

DAPHNE A wedding present from us?

BILL No problem about your flowers, we'll send you ours. Yes Tim remembered to get ours alright. (*Laughs. Then to the others.*) He's not laughing. (*To phone.*) We'll put them in a taxi and send them straight round to the Church. Yes. Goodbye.

DAPHNE What was that about our present being a kitten?

TIMOTHY First things, first. We've got to get these flowers over to the Church.

(TIMOTHY *starts to unpin* DAPHNE'*s spray as* JUDY *and* URSULA *enter. They are both now fully dressed for the wedding.*)

DAPHNE (*resisting*) Is this absolutely necessary?

JUDY (*as she enters*) Good Lord Mummy, it's not all that serious.

URSULA Well he shouted at me.

JUDY — I'm sure he's sorry. (*To* TIMOTHY.) You're sorry aren't you, Daddy.

TIMOTHY — Yes the Babcock's will never forgive me.

URSULA — (*as* TIM *removes her flower*) What on earth are you doing now?

TIMOTHY — Collecting flowers.

BILL — We're sending ours over to the Babcocks.

URSULA — What?

BILL — This is no day to be upsetting your millionaire-in-laws.

TIMOTHY — (*crossing to* JUDY *with the flowers he's so far collected*) That'll do for Nicholas, that'll do for Mrs Babcock. . . (*Plucking rose from* JUDY'*s posy.*) That'll do for Mr Babcock. . .

JUDY — (*protesting*) Daddy!

TIMOTHY — Don't be selfish, darling, you've got such a lot there.

BILL — Where are the rest of the flowers?

URSULA — In the hall.

BILL — Good. I'll get them together and shove them all into a taxi. Tim, you get yourself dressed, you've got to get off to the Church.

(BILL *starts to go.*)

DAPHNE — I thought it was an electric blanket.

(BILL *stops and everyone turns slowly to look at her.*)

It must have been Gerald's idea to give them a kitten.

URSULA — Kitten?

BILL — Oh, God.

TIMOTHY Bill, I think I'd better tell them about Polly.

URSULA
JUDY } (*together*) Polly?

BILL Yes, Polly's the new kitten. (*Hopefully, to* TIMOTHY.) We haven't lost her have we?

TIMOTHY No. I've put her in the er – (*Nods towards dining room.*) with the other presents.

JUDY Honestly Daddy, what's the matter with you?

TIMOTHY Just a bit of a problem.

URSULA And don't bother to say how gorgeous your daughter looks will you?

TIMOTHY No – I mean gorgeous. I haven't seen that dress before have I?

URSULA What would you do with him?

BILL Get him changed. Come on Ursula, give me a hand. (*Takes button holes from* TIM.)

(*During the ensuing pages they take off his casual clothes and dress him in his morning suit.*)

TIMOTHY What about Polly?

BILL She'll be alright. We'll leave her a ball of wool and a saucer of milk.

(GERALD *enters now fully dressed, holding up his trousers to show his socks which are light blue.*)

GERALD Best I could do I'm afraid. D'you think anyone'll notice?

DAPHNE Of course they will. Go and change them at once.

GERALD Yes dear. Hello. . . hello! Why are you de-bagging Timothy?

BILL Never mind. Judy, you take over here. I'll get the rest of the flowers, sir, and you can take them round in a taxi.

GERALD Flowers? Taxi? What?

BILL You're going to Babcock.

(BILL *exits.* GERALD *starts to follow, then stops.*)

GERALD Where's that?

DAPHNE Infuriating man. (*Loudly.*) Mr Babcock, at the Church.

GERALD Is he the Vicar?

JUDY Nicholas's father.

GERALD Oh, him.

DAPHNE And I want to know why you changed your mind about that electric blanket.

GERALD (*blankly*) What?

DAPHNE And I hope our present's going to be alright in there.

GERALD Our present? In there?

DAPHNE The kitten.

GERALD Our present, the kitten? In there?

(*He goes to the dining room door and opens it to have a look.*)

TIMOTHY Don't do that! Gerald! Don't go in there...

(TIMOTHY *takes a step from between* JUDY *and* URSULA *and trips on his trousers as* POLLY *enters.* TIMOTHY *hastily tries to pull his trousers up in front of* POLLY.)

TIMOTHY I'm terribly sorry. I really am, most terribly sorry.

URSULA There's no need to go on about it, dear, mother's seen your knees before.

TIMOTHY I know but Polly hasn't.

DAPHNE (*looking towards dining room*) Polly?

GERALD (*also looking*) Polly?

(BILL *enters with box of flowers.*)

BILL Off you go with these, sir, we'll find you a taxi.

GERALD (*takes the box*) Most unwise, you know, most unwise.

BILL What is?

GERALD A kitten and a parrot they'll tear each other to pieces.

(*He exits with* BILL.)

BILL (*as he goes*) Parrot?

TIMOTHY (*struggling with his clothes, whispering to* POLLY) You'd better come with me to the Church.

URSULA I beg your pardon?

TIMOTHY Er – I said you better come with me to the Church.

URSULA Yes. I am coming with you.

TIMOTHY Good I'm just checking, that's all. (*Whispering to* POLLY.) Then I can talk to you properly.

DAPHNE What?

TIMOTHY (*still whispering*) I said I can't talk properly.

DAPHNE (*to* URSULA) What is the matter with the man?

URSULA I don't know mother. Give me his waistcoat, Judy.

POLLY As long as I can sit next to you.

TIMOTHY Yes, I'd like that.

DAPHNE You'd like what?

TIMOTHY (*to* DAPHNE) I'd like to sit next to you.

DAPHNE Sit next to me?

TIMOTHY Yes, at the Church. Then I can hold hands with you, too.

DAPHNE Now I *know* he's cracking up.

URSULA Come on, darling, put your shoes on.

(BILL *enters.*)

BILL Hurry up for God's sake. The cars'll be here any minute.

DAPHNE Well I'm ready.

BILL We'll nip down through the park and pick up our flowers in Knightsbridge somewhere.

URSULA Yes.

POLLY Pick them from the Park.

TIMOTHY (*laughing*) Pick them from the Park –

(*He stops laughing when he realises everyone is looking at him.*)

TIMOTHY That was Polly.

BILL (*trying to laugh it off casually*) Oh, has that damn kitten got out again?

DAPHNE I could have sworn it was a blanket.

URSULA Look darling, can't we sort Polly out after the wedding.

TIMOTHY No, she might be gone by then.

DAPHNE Well, put some butter on her paws.

TIMOTHY (*to* BILL) No Bill, she's got to come with me, she'll fret by herself.

POLLY
URSULA } (*together*) Oooooh, thank you. If you don't leave at once you needn't come at all.

(POLLY *kisses him as* JUDY *takes* URSULA *aside.*)

DAPHNE You should have spoken to him like that twenty years ago.

JUDY Mummy for heaven's sake, it's a very emotional day for Daddy.

TIMOTHY (*coming out of the kiss*) Oh, what a kiss.

(*The ladies turn and see* BILL *standing by* TIMOTHY. BILL *tries to shrug off the situation, with* TIM *clinging to him for support.*)

TIMOTHY I'm still wobbling, Bill.

BILL Let's go.

TIMOTHY Where are you taking me?

BILL St. Barnabas.

TIMOTHY No, Bill, I can't leave Polly.

BILL You've got to.

TIMOTHY But what if she's got to go?

DAPHNE Open a window and put down some newspaper.

POLLY Newspaper!?

(TIMOTHY *goes to* POLLY.)

TIMOTHY Would you mind waiting in there a second.

DAPHNE I'll do no such thing!

TIMOTHY Not you! (*He ushers* POLLY *into the dining room gesticulating for her to keep quiet and shuts the door.*)

URSULA (*to* BILL) What's he doing?

TIMOTHY (*chuckling*) Open a window and put down some newspaper. (*Seeing their faces.*) It's no use Bill, I'll have to tell them.

BILL (*desperate*) No, please, don't do it.

TIMOTHY It's alright, Ursula will understand.

BILL She won't.

TIMOTHY She will.

BILL She won't.

TIMOTHY She might.

BILL She won't.

URSULA Try me!

TIMOTHY (*to* BILL) There you are, she wants me to try her.

BILL Alright, try her.

TIMOTHY Yes, I'll try her. Look I know you're going to think I'm mad, well, anybody would think I was mad. Bill thinks I'm mad, and . . . (*To* DAPHNE.) I know what you think. Don't ask me to explain, because I can't explain. It's never happened to anyone before. And at first I wasn't sure that it was happening to me, but it is.

BILL Oh, you're doing very well.

JUDY What is it, Daddy?

URSULA It's five to twelve, that's what it is.

TIMOTHY I'm sorry, darling. I wouldn't have chosen today but it chose me, or rather she did. Or perhaps I chose her, its very difficult to say which came first. It's rather like the thing about the chicken and the egg.

(*They all stare at him.*)

BILL Keep going, son.

(*Goes to pour a drink for* DAPHNE, *which he gives her, then pours one for* JUDY *and* URSULA.)

URSULA Darling, who chose you?

TIMOTHY Polly.

DAPHNE The kitten?

TIMOTHY No! Not that Polly, *my* Polly.

JUDY Your Polly.

TIMOTHY Yes, She's a young lady.

URSULA Are you telling me you're having an affair?

TIMOTHY No – yes – no. Well it depends what you mean by an affair.

DAPHNE I told you, twenty years ago you couldn't trust him.

URSULA How long has it been going on?

TIMOTHY (*looks at watch*) About fifteen minutes.

URSULA Fifteen minutes?

BILL Don't worry, there's more to come.

(*Hands glass to* URSULA *and* JUDY.)

TIMOTHY You see, I met her this morning.

URSULA This morning.

TIMOTHY That's right.

JUDY Where?

TIMOTHY Behind the sofa.

DAPHNE The sofa? (*Gulps down her drink.*)

TIMOTHY There was absolutely no problem at all until she kissed me.

URSULA (*flatly*) Lovely.

DAPHNE (*aside to* URSULA) Didn't I always say, the eyes too close together.

TIMOTHY I tried to tell her to go, but after she kissed me I had no control over it.

DAPHNE (*to* BILL) I warned her about that too.

JUDY What was she doing behind the sofa in the first place?

TIMOTHY Ah, well, that's the point you see, there's something rather unusual about this girl.

BILL Hold very tight, please.

TIMOTHY You see, for some inexplicable reason nobody else but me can see her.

(*There is another stunned silence.*)

BILL That's gone down a treat.

TIMOTHY The funny thing was I'd just been telling Bill about my idea for taking the flop out of flappers, and the next minute there she was, with a little hat, short hair, big feather boa, beads, the lot.

URSULA (*gently*) Now Timothy, darling –

BILL He'll be alright, he banged his head on the door.

DAPHNE Oh. (*Puts glass down.*)

URSULA Look, let's get hold of a doctor.

TIMOTHY Doctor?

URSULA To give you a sedative. It's all been too much for you. Work, wedding, Mr Babcock, Perkins Bra's – catering manager–

TIMOTHY I don't need a doctor.

BILL I told you to keep quiet about it.

URSULA You've had a nasty bang on the head and now you're seeing things.

TIMOTHY I haven't just been seeing her, I've been feeling her as well.

DAPHNE Really!

URSULA Mother, please. (*To* TIMOTHY.) It's all those pills you take.

DAPHNE Nonsense! It's a common or garden hallucination. Gerald had a patient once who got kicked in the head by a horse. Spent the next forty-eight hours talking about it to Lady Godiva.

BILL But he fully recovered?

DAPHNE Oh, he's fine. Runs a riding school near Coventry.

(GERALD *enters from the hall, still carrying the flowers.*)

GERALD I'm not too clear Daphne. What kitten?

DAPHNE Hmm?

GERALD When I was going out just now, someone said some crazy thing about a kitten.

BILL You should've stayed, it got better.

DAPHNE Haven't you got rid of those flowers yet, dear?

GERALD I was going to, but then I remembered someone said something about a kitten. And I could've sworn it was a blanket.

BILL Oh, don't you start!

DAPHNE Look, let's all get to the Church and forget about this Polly.

GERALD Yes. Polly?

DAPHNE The kitten.

GERALD Oh, it's a kitten. I thought it was a parrot.

DAPHNE Gerald, will you please go and put those flowers in a taxi.

GERALD No need for a taxi now.

DAPHNE Why not?

GERALD The cars have been here for the last five minutes.

DAPHNE Oh Ursula look at the time.

URSULA Right, let's get to the Church. All we have to do is decide who stays here with Timothy until the doctor arrives.

TIMOTHY Doctor?

URSULA Now who can we spare to look after him. I suppose you'd better go to the Church, Judy, otherwise it'll look rude. (*To* BILL.) Bill, you're probably the best one to stay because no one will miss you.

BILL Thank you.

JUDY I can't go without Daddy.

URSULA I know it's not ideal.

BILL He's supposed to be giving Judy away.

JUDY Yes.

URSULA (*to* JUDY) Don't worry there must be somebody there who can give you away.

DAPHNE I think it'd be safer if we gave your father away.

URSULA Why don't you wait in one of the cars while we sort it out.

(URSULA *hustles* JUDY *out of the room, then returns.*)

BILL Surely he can have a sedative and a doctor after the reception. You can't have a wedding without the bride's father.

TIMOTHY I want to come and I know Polly would enjoy it.

URSULA (*making a decision*) Alright. Fine. If she's going to enjoy it, bring her.

TIMOTHY Thank you darling. (*Goes and opens the dining room door and calls out.*) Polly.

URSULA Father?

GERALD (*coming to*) That's me.

URSULA Get in one of the cars and take those flowers to St. Barnabas.

GERALD St. Barnabas. Right.

(*He notices* TIMOTHY *gesticulating for* POLLY *to come in . . .*)

GERALD (*to* TIMOTHY) Still directing the traffic I see.

(GERALD *exits as* POLLY *comes in from the dining room.*)

TIMOTHY Polly, now you've met my partner, Bill Shorter. This is my wife Ursula and this is my mother-in-law, Mrs Drimmond.

POLLY (*to* URSULA) Hello. (*She sits beside* DAPHNE *on the sofa.*) Hello.

(*There is a pause.*)

BILL (*aside to* URSULA) Just a quick hand shake will do.

URSULA (*shaking hands with thin air*) How do you do.

TIMOTHY No darling, she's not there.

URSULA Well, where is she then?

TIMOTHY She's sitting next to Daphne.

DAPHNE (*jumping up*) Ahh!

URSULA Mother!

TIMOTHY Polly, it's all been fixed, you can come with us to the Church.

POLLY Oh scrumptious.

(*She throws her arms round* TIMOTHY *and kisses him. He gets the same silly dazed look on his face.*)

BILL Look out, I think he's gone wobbly again.

(*The phone rings.* BILL *picks it up and hands it straight to* TIMOTHY.)

It's for you.

TIMOTHY (*on phone*) Hello, wobbly here. I mean, Timothy Westerby. – Oh, hello, Mr Babcock, don't worry about the flowers because my father-in-law's on his way – beg your pardon? – Oh. (*To the others.*) he says never mind the bloody flowers, where the bloody hell are *we*?

BILL It's a bloody good question.

POLLY Language.

TIMOTHY Sorry Polly – I mean Mr Babcock.

(BILL *takes the phone quickly.*)

BILL Hello sir, it's Bill Shorter again – No, no he wasn't calling you Polly, it was that damned kitten again – (*To the others.*) He wants to know what the hell I'm talking about.

URSULA (*takes phone from* BILL) Hello Charles, Ursula here. Haven't we chosen a gorgeous day for it – Yes, there has been a slight delay. It seems that Timothy's broken his leg a little.

DAPHNE Ursula! (*Grabs the phone.*)

TIMOTHY Broken my leg a little?

BILL Quiet!

DAPHNE (*on phone*) Hello, it's Mrs Drimmond here now. Look, as soon as you and Nicholas get to the Church. . .(*The blistering answer at the other end of the phone causes* DAPHNE *to hold the receiver away from her ear.*) Cor! (*To the others.*) They're at the Church, he's speaking from the vestry. (*Into phone.*) No, I'm afraid Ursula was right, it's a very nasty break...

TIMOTHY A very nasty...?

BILL Quiet!

DAPHNE (*on phone*) Yes it's a triple compound fracture.

TIMOTHY Triple compound –?

DAPHNE (*to* TIMOTHY, *very loudly*) Quiet! (*Then quickly into phone.*) No, not you, Mr Babcock. What was that? (*All smiles.*) He was getting into one of the cars when he tripped over something...That bloody kitten? Yes, very likely. Funny, I could have sworn it was a blanket! (*Another blistering remark at the other end of the phone.*) That must be an Australian word! (*Replaces receiver.*)

(JUDY *enters with her veil now on, and carrying her posy.*)

JUDY Does anybody know which of the cars I'm going in?

URSULA Surely the drivers know.

JUDY They thought they did but Grandad started organising things.

URSULA It doesn't matter which one you go in, because they're all going to St. Barnabas.

JUDY I wouldn't bank on it. Grandad keeps calling it Dr Barnados.

URSULA Come on, mother, and you, Bill.

BILL Judy, you grab hold of your father and get him into the second car.

JUDY (*delighted*) Oh, you're coming.

TIMOTHY Course, I'm coming.

JUDY Smashing.

TIMOTHY And so's Polly.

JUDY Polly?

TIMOTHY Yes, you haven't met her, have –

BILL (*interrupting*) Introduce her in the car.

TIMOTHY Good idea, Bill.

JUDY You mean she's coming with us?

URSULA Yes.

JUDY I'm not walking down the aisle with Daddy and his dream girl.

URSULA Please darling, don't be difficult.

POLLY Don't worry we'll sit at the back of the Church.

TIMOTHY There you are. Did you hear that.

ALL No!

TIMOTHY Polly says she and I can sit at the back of the Church.

JUDY You're supposed to be up front with me and the Vicar.

BILL Tell you what we'll bung her in with the bridesmaids.

TIMOTHY (*affronted*) Bung her in with the bridesmaids!

POLLY Oh, don't excite yourself Timothy Royston.

(*During the next few lines,* URSULA, DAPHNE *and* JUDY *stare at* TIMOTHY *who appears to them to be carrying on a one-sided conversation.*)

TIMOTHY They don't appreciate you Polly.

POLLY — Well it can't be easy for them.

TIMOTHY — What a sweet, kind, understanding girl you are – (*To the others.*) Have you ever met such a girl? No, of course you haven't. She's absolutely marvellous, she's so innocent and pure. (*To* URSULA.) She's just like our Judy. (JUDY *turns away.*) And after the service she's coming back here for the reception.

POLLY — (*delighted*) Oh, simmer me in prune juice!

TIMOTHY — (*suddenly laughing*) Oh, simmer her in prune juice. She's going to keep us all in stitches. This drive to the Church, Judy, is going to be a riot.

(JUDY *bursts into tears and runs out of the room.*)

BILL — Well, there goes the bride.

DAPHNE — (*to* TIMOTHY) Now look what you've done!

POLLY — I'm terribly sorry Timothy.

TIMOTHY — That's alright Polly, wasn't your fault.

DAPHNE — Of course it wasn't my fault.

TIMOTHY — Not you. Polly was just saying –

URSULA — Can't you keep that damn girl quiet.

TIMOTHY — She was only saying how sorry –

URSULA — (*looking in the wrong direction*) Well don't say it again.

TIMOTHY — That's no way to speak to a guest.

URSULA — Well she's not my guest.

TIMOTHY — Doesn't matter whose guest she is, she's in our house. Come on Polly we'll find Judy and sort it out.

URSULA — I think you better let Bill go and sort this out.

TIMOTHY No, this is a father's job.

BILL Well leave your Polly Perkins here with me.

TIMOTHY I'll do no such thing. If you're looking for a new bottom to pinch, try Daphne's.

(*Exits with* POLLY.)

DAPHNE What?

BILL Don't worry, Ursula, I'll sort it out.

URSULA (*handing* BILL TIM'*s discarded clothes*) Could you put these in Timothy's room?

BILL Right.

DAPHNE Does his sort of thing run in your husband's family?

URSULA I don't think so.

DAPHNE What were his father and mother like?

BILL Careless – very careless.

(*He exits with the clothes.*)

DAPHNE Judy should have been saying "I will" three minutes ago.

URSULA Oh dear.

(GERALD *enters still carrying the flowers.*)

GERALD Are you lot coming or not?

URSULA Haven't you gone yet, dear?

GERALD I've been arguing with those driver chappies.

URSULA But you should be at the Church.

GERALD That's what they're saying. They've got a funeral this afternoon.

URSULA Mr Babcock's still waiting.

DAPHNE He'll be having a blue fit.

GERALD (*referring to his socks*) Yes, I think so. They're not bad at all, actually.

DAPHNE Forty years I've had of this.

GERALD D'you want me to change them?

URSULA
DAPHNE } (*together*) No!

GERALD Right, Timothy had better lead the way. Where is he by the way?

URSULA Coming on later.

DAPHNE Or possibly not at all.

GERALD (*stopping*) Not at all? Dammit he's Judy's father.

DAPHNE He's gone and had a breakdown.

GERALD (*misunderstanding her*) Can't we pick him up in our car?

DAPHNE Gerald! Get in to one of those cars and go. Someone's got to represent this family at the wedding, and God help us, it looks as though it's got to be you. (*Pushes him towards hall.*)

URSULA We must get a doctor as soon as it's over.

DAPHNE Yes.

GERALD What was that?

DAPHNE They'll need a doctor.

GERALD Oh. (*Starts to go, then stops and turns.*) I'm a doctor.

URSULA
DAPHNE } (*together*) Out!

(GERALD *starts to go as* TIMOTHY *enters.*)

TIMOTHY It's no use. I can't do a thing about it.

GERALD Get the A.A. to send a breakdown van.

URSULA
DAPHNE } (*together*) Out!

(GERALD *exits.* TIMOTHY *starts to follow but is called back.*)

DAPHNE Not you, Timothy.

URSULA Where's Judy now?

TIMOTHY In her room having hysterics. It's alright. Bill's up there trying to calm her down.

DAPHNE This was supposed to be the happiest day of her life.

TIMOTHY I must say Polly was being as nice as pie –

URSULA You tell Polly to keep her little beak out of this – (*Rounding on thin air.*) If you hadn't turned up today my girl –

TIMOTHY Darling.

URSULA (*ignoring him*) Our daughter would have been –

TIMOTHY Darling she's not there.

URSULA (*changing direction*) Our daughter would've been happily –

TIMOTHY Please darling. She's not there either. She's out in the hall, waiting for us.

DAPHNE None of this would've happened if it hadn't been for your damned Polly.

TIMOTHY Now that's not fair. She didn't realise she was coming on an awkward day.

URSULA Don't tell me she didn't realise. Of course she realised.

DAPHNE Don't get excited, Ursula.

URSULA She's got a hell of a nerve kissing you in front of me and doing god knows what behind the sofa.

TIMOTHY She hasn't done a thing yet except wobble a bit when I kiss her.

URSULA I didn't know girls found you so irresistable.

TIMOTHY And why shouldn't they find me irresistable.

DAPHNE I can give you a few reasons.

TIMOTHY You keep quiet. (*To* URSULA.) You found me irresistable once.

URSULA Yes, twenty years ago.

TIMOTHY And that was the last time you had a good look at me, What colour are my eyes?

URSULA Oh, don't be ridiculous.

TIMOTHY No, come on. (*Shuts his eyes.*) What colour?

URSULA Blue, I think.

TIMOTHY You only think.

URSULA Yes blue.

TIMOTHY But have you ever noticed anything unusual about them?

DAPHNE Too close together.

(TIMOTHY *opens his eyes and glares at* DAPHNE.)

TIMOTHY In a certain light, they change colour from blue to grey. Polly spotted it immediately, and my smile. Not to mention my stern looks.

URSULA Honestly, flattery gets them everywhere.

DAPHNE Ursula's been far too busy running a home and bringing up Judy to notice how your eyes change, Or how your stern looks.

(TIMOTHY *glares at her.*)

TIMOTHY That's my point, She should've made sure she wasn't too busy. (*Points to the hall.*) Out there's a beautiful young girl who recognised at once all my endearing qualities.

URSULA Typical. You run me down and stick up for some young tart who picked you up at –

TIMOTHY (*cutting in*) Tart?

URSULA Well what else?

DAPHNE Don't let him upset you, Ursula. This wretched girl only exists in his mind.

URSULA Yes, a pretty filthy one.

TIMOTHY Polly is not a tart. She's a very outgoing girl with a beautiful nature.

DAPHNE It's not a doctor you need, Ursula, its a divorce.

TIMOTHY And what's more, she adores Royston.

DAPHNE Then the sooner she goes back there the better.

TIMOTHY It's my middle name. When she says Timothy Royston Westerby, she makes it sound like The Great Ghengis Khan.

URSULA Well she's in for a bit of a disappointment when she discovers the Great Ghengis Can't.

TIMOTHY (*stung*) Oh, thank you. Thank you very much indeed. I suppose the whole of our married life is going to be trotted out as evidence is it? Well, you'll be alright. (*Indicates* DAPHNE.) You've got the Hanging Judge on your side.

(BILL *enters.*)

BILL It's no good she won't listen to me.

DAPHNE Stupid child.

BILL She's locked her door and refuses to come out.

DAPHNE What a wedding.

URSULA You don't think the Vicar could come here do you?

DAPHNE Course not. Go and drag her out Ursula.

BILL Waste of time, Tim's the only one she'll talk to.

TIMOTHY I'd better go up – the poor little thing.

DAPHNE Poor little thing? The girl's unbalanced. (*Eyeing* TIMOTHY.) And it certainly doesn't come from our side of the family.

TIMOTHY (*to* URSULA) Would you remind me again, Ursula, how charming your mother can be. I keep forgetting.

URSULA There's no need to be rude to Daphne.

TIMOTHY She was rude to me and so were you.

URSULA I was not. I'm just upset at the way this girl seems to have taken you over.

TIMOTHY You attacked me personally.

URSULA I did not.

TIMOTHY You did. (*To* BILL.) She did, Bill. She said my Ghengis Couldn't.

URSULA Well it isn't so far removed from the truth.

TIMOTHY There you go again. (*To* DAPHNE.) Judge Jeffery's already got the black cap on. What your daughter means is that once in a blue moon I happen to come home emotionally and physically exhausted. Now I'd like you to ask her why that always seems to coincide with the one night in the year she decided to throw her nightie out of the window and swing from the chandelier.

URSULA Oh! You do exaggerate.

BILL Get upstairs to Judy.

(He pushes TIM *towards the door as* GERALD *bursts in. He is breathless.)*

GERALD *(to* TIMOTHY*)* Ah, did you get your car fixed.

TIMOTHY Yes, thanks I did. *(Goes to exit, realises, returns.)* What car?

DAPHNE OUT!

(He exits. GERALD *moves in.)*

BILL Look here, sir, what are you doing back here?

GERALD *(puffing)* Vicar – vicar – vicar –

DAPHNE Stop repeating yourself, dear.

GERALD Babcock – Babcock –

DAPHNE Gerald!

GERALD Things are getting violent in the Vestry.

DAPHNE Now what is happening Gerald?

GERALD Mr Babcock and the Vicar. In the Vestry.

URSULA Yes, but what about them?

GERALD I hate to say it but he actually lost his temper.

URSULA What, the Vicar?

GERALD No, Mr Babcock. And a string of the most shocking language.

BILL That's Babcock.

GERALD — No that was the Vicar. You see, my arrival didn't seem to do the trick with Babcock. He seemed a bit upset when three limousines rolled up and only me and flowers got out.

DAPHNE — But why on earth did you take all three cars?

GERALD — I didn't. I got in the first one and other two followed.

BILL — Yes, but why?

GERALD — That's exactly what I asked them when we got to the Church. Apparently they mistook my farewell wave for a signal to advance. I still think Babcock behaved very badly taking it out on the Vicar. He stormed into the Vestry and grabbed him by the hassock.

(*They all look at him.*)

BILL — I'm not surprised he used shocking language.

(GERALD *chuckles.*)

DAPHNE — It's cassock, Gerald.

GERALD — Oh, is it? Oh, well maybe that's what upset him. I've been calling him Babcock.

(*The phone rings,* BILL, URSULA *and* DAPHNE *all exchange a nervous glance, none of them wishing to get involved with* BABCOCK.)

BILL — There he is again.

GERALD — I'm not afraid of him.

(*He moves to pick up the receiver.*)

DAPHNE — No. (*Pulls him back.*)

GERALD — (*startled*) What did you do that for?

DAPHNE — You've caused enough chaos today.

GERALD I'll smooth things over, don't worry. (*Goes to phone.*) Just listen to this. (*Lifts the receiver.*) Hello there. Dr Drimmond speaking. Now in the first place I want to apologise for calling you Babcock, Mr Cassock. And in the second place...

BILL For God's sake don't go on to the second place.

(*He grabs the phone from* GERALD *and speaks without pausing.*)

Hello Babcock. Shorter here. Quite understand your feelings. That Vicar's enough to make anyone blow their top. But it's his "holier than thou" attitude that sticks in my – I beg your pardon? – (*To* URSULA.) It is the Vicar.

(*He hands her the telephone.*)

URSULA (*sweetly*) Good morning, Vicar, you've just caught me. I was just getting into the car – what wedding? Oh the wedding, yes, we're all on our way – well we would have been if you hadn't called us back to answer the phone – Oh tell the organist three minutes at the most. (*Puts her hand over the mouthpiece.*) He's already been twice through his canticles. (*On phone.*) Alright vicar, goodbye.

(TIMOTHY *enters with* POLLY. *He looks very upset and agitated.*)

BILL Have you done the trick with Judy?

TIMOTHY No I have not!

URSULA Well, we've had the Vicar on the telephone now and he's expecting us in three minutes.

TIMOTHY Get the vicar on the telephone again and tell him that your daughter has decided not to go to the Church at all today.

URSULA What?

DAPHNE } *(together)* I don't believe it.
BILL } Hells bells.

TIMOTHY She says it's a Registry Office or nothing.

GERALD What did he say?

URSULA I hope you and Polly are pleased with yourselves.

TIMOTHY It's not a question of Polly and Timothy – it's a question of Judy and Virginity.

GERALD Holy Trinity? I thought it was Barnabas.

TIMOTHY She says she's not getting married in Church in white, because the whole thing would be hypocrisy.

DAPHNE Nonsense! All young brides get married in white.

TIMOTHY Not when the bride has already been seduced by the groom!

GERALD Shouldn't we be pushing off. I'm a bit worried about leaving the Vicar alone with Mr Cassock.

DAPHNE The wedding's off. Don't you ever hear anything.

GERALD Oh, is it? What a pity. (*Looks at his suit.*) I wonder if there's a meeting at Ascot, or somewhere. (*Goes to refill his champagne glass.*)

TIMOTHY It's a fine thing for a father to discover on his daughter's wedding day. I thought she was chaste.

BILL Well, she certainly got caught.

(POLLY *laughs and sits on the floor.* D.S. *centre to watch everyone.*)

TIMOTHY Polly please. It's nothing to laugh at.

BILL I'm glad someone appreciated it.

TIMOTHY (*moves to* BILL) You've never had a daughter.

BILL Good God, it's not all that serious.

TIMOTHY Not serious. She's barely twenty and already deflowered.

GERALD No I delivered those alright.

DAPHNE Gerald.

(TIMOTHY *moves to* URSULA, *stepping over* POLLY. GERALD *reacts to* TIMOTHY *apparently stepping over nothing.*)

TIMOTHY A Registry Office is the only fit place for those two.

DAPHNE You can't get four hundred – people into a Registry Office.

(TIMOTHY *moves back to* DAPHNE *stepping over* POLLY. GERALD *reacts again.*)

TIMOTHY Well, I don't care. I only knew seventeen of them anyway.

DAPHNE She's got to get married today.

TIMOTHY Oh, pregnant as well is she?

DAPHNE You have spent the best part of £3,000 on this wedding. What are you going to do about the Reception, the photographers, the Champagne, the waiters –

BILL To say nothing of the sixteen hundred prawn-vol-au-vents.

TIMOTHY That can all go ahead. The last people to be missed are the bride and groom.

URSULA I warned Judy not to tell you.

(TIMOTHY *crosses back to* URSULA *stepping over* POLLY. GERALD *is now finding this step quite amusing.)*

TIMOTHY Oh! You warned Judy not to tell me. You didn't warn me did you? So you knew all about it, did you?

URSULA Yes. And I knew exactly what you'd do about it.

TIMOTHY And what was that, might I ask? (*Putting his hands on his hips.*)

URSULA Stand there shouting with your hands on your hips.

TIMOTHY (*shouting*) I am not shouting and I have not got my hands on my... (*He stops shouting and quickly takes his hands off his hips.*) Oh!

BILL Look, Tim, I think there are more important things –

(TIMOTHY *crosses to* BILL, *stepping over* POLLY, *with* GERALD *joining in the fun doing the step in unison.*)

TIMOTHY (*flaring up*) Oh, yes, it might not seem important to a man of your low habits.

BILL (*politely*) Thank you.

(TIMOTHY *crosses to* URSULA, *but this time he doesn't have to step over* POLLY'*s legs, because she has pulled them in.* GERALD *starts to do the little step and is very disappointed to see that* TIMOTHY *has omitted to do it.*)

TIMOTHY (*to* URSULA) But I happen to have some old fashioned standards, Ursula, and the sooner you realise it...

(GERALD *interrupts him by tapping him on the shoulder.*)

GERALD Hang on, you haven't done the little do-dah. (*He mimes the little step.*)

TIMOTHY (*blankly*) The what?

GERALD The little do-dah.

(GERALD *does it once more and* TIMOTHY *decides to ignore him.*)

TIMOTHY (*to* GERALD, *pointing to the glass in his hand*) I should lay off that stuff if I were you. Listen, Ursula, I've got some very old fashioned standards –

URSULA There you go again, shouting and –

TIMOTHY I am not shou – (*He stops himself again and takes his hands off his hips. Then, to* POLLY.) You can see what I have to put up with. Have you ever met such a family?

POLLY They don't seem too bad.

TIMOTHY (*pressing on*) No, of course you haven't. People didn't behave like this in the 1920's.

GERALD (*puzzled*) Who's he talking to?

DAPHNE
URSULA } (*together*) Polly!

GERALD (*looking around the floor*) Oh. Puss, puss, puss, puss, puss!

DAPHNE Will you come away? This is a madhouse.

(*She pushes* GERALD *off and they exit.*)

TIMOTHY (*to* POLLY) You see the sort of females I've got surrounding me. My mother-in-law's a dragon, my wife sides with everyone except her husband and my daughter's a nymphomaniac.

BILL I'd hardly call a little pre-marital –

TIMOTHY Little? She's just been telling me up there –

URSULA I told her not to.

TIMOTHY They couldn't have done it more often if they'd been on a productivity bonus.

URSULA Well better late than never. Nicholas is marrying her now.

TIMOTHY If you think I'm going to stand by in Church while the Vicar blesses that vile rapist...

POLLY Oh, calm down Timothy Royston.

TIMOTHY You wouldn't understand a father's feelings, Polly.

BILL He's off again.

TIMOTHY (*to* POLLY) Young people didn't behave like that in the Twenties, did they?

POLLY Don't know.

TIMOTHY No, of course they didn't. A girl was put on a pedestal then, and looked up to. Escorts arrived in top hat and tails, and used to dance all night at Romano's. You saw all those Hollywood musicals, didn't you?

BILL Hollywood musicals?

TIMOTHY Yes, with Fred Astaire and Ginger Rogers. The only thing Fred ever jumped on was the furniture.

URSULA But we're not living in the Twenties now.

TIMOTHY More's the pity, because a girl was really wooed then, with soft lights and music and violins, and stage door Johnnies at the Tivoli, drinking champagne out of the girl's slippers. I tell you, Bill, a girl was a goddess then.

URSULA Yes, but with pretty soggy feet–

TIMOTHY Perhaps you'd be good enough to look after Polly while I go and get changed.

URSULA But you *are* changed.

TIMOTHY Changed back, I mean. Nothing would induce me to go through with this wedding now.

URSULA } (*together*) Oh, Timothy!
BILL } For heaven's sake –

TIMOTHY No. My mind's made up (*Indicating* POLLY.) This lovely young creature has made me realise what a sordid society we're living in today.

(*He turns to go into the hall, as* GERALD *opens the double doors.*)

GERALD Ursula, where's...

(*As the door opens, it hits* TIMOTHY *on the head, and he collapses into the armchair.* BILL *and* URSULA *go to him.*)

GERALD (*rubbing his knuckles*) You must get this door fixed, you know. Keeps sticking. (*Suddenly sees* TIM.) Who's that?

URSULA (*patting* TIM*'s cheeks*) Timothy!

GERALD Poor old chap. (*Goes to* URSULA.) Probably exhausted himself with all those little do-dah's. (*Moves away, doing the little jump.*)

BILL (*to* TIM) Are you alright, old man?

GERALD By the way, Mr Alcock's downstairs. I've left him in the hall. (*Takes off his tailcoat and puts it on the sofa.*)

BILL Alcock?

GERALD Nicholas's father.

BILL & URSULA Mr Babcock.

GERALD Very likely.

URSULA Timothy! Timothy, are you alright?

TIMOTHY (*coming round*) Oh, um...

URSULA Oh, thank goodness you've come round.

TIMOTHY (*getting to his feet*) Oh yes, I love coming round. (*Sees* URSULA.) How are you? How nice to see you again. What a great pleasure. I'm sorry, but I'm afraid you'll have to remind me...

URSULA Remind you?

TIMOTHY Yes, I know your face, but I can't put a name to it.

BILL (*tentatively*) Now, now, gently does it.

TIMOTHY (*turning, brightly*) Ah, hello. You must be the Catering Manager.

BILL Catering Manager.

TIMOTHY (*looking around*) Very nice of you to greet us like this. I must say you've done it all quite beautifully. What do you think of the Savoy, Polly?

BILL Savoy?

POLLY Oh, peachy poos.

TIMOTHY (*chuckles*) Peachy poos! (*Noticing* GERALD.) Ah, porter. You'll find our luggage out there at Reception. Just take the bags up to the Bridal Suite, will you?

(*He tips* GERALD *a £1 coin.* GERALD *exits, somewhat puzzled.*)

(*Turning to* BILL.) Now I know it's not really your Department, but you might try and get my car in the garage, will you?

BILL Your car?

TIMOTHY You can't miss it, it's the very latest Rolls.

BILL Very latest?

TIMOTHY Yes, 1926.

URSULA
BILL } (*together*) 1926!

TIMOTHY (*returning to* POLLY) Then whenever you're ready, I'll sign the Register, and carry my bride into the bedroom.

(BILL *and* URSULA *gape at each other, as* DAPHNE *enters.*)

DAPHNE Ursula, we women have got to take a firm stand!

TIMOTHY Mrs Pankhurst. How nice to see you!

DAPHNE Aaah! (*She turns and rushes off.*)

(BLACKOUT)

ACT TWO

The scene is the same—The action continuous.

BILL (*slowly*) Did you say carry your bride into the bedroom?

TIMOTHY That's the jolly old idea, yes.

URSULA Timothy.

TIMOTHY (*looking round*) Timothy?

URSULA Don't you think you'd better –

TIMOTHY (*cutting in*) Introduce myself, of course. Royston Westerby.

URSULA Royston?

TIMOTHY Yes. (*Takes her hand and kisses it.*) Enchante Madam. Have you been staying at the Savoy long?

URSULA Just arrived.

TIMOTHY I know we've met somewhere. Wasn't last Tuesday at Romano's was it?

URSULA (*staring blankly*) What?

TIMOTHY Bunty Pinkerton's Twenty First. (*To Polly.*) Marvellous do, wasn't it?

POLLY Ripping.

BILL (*trying to be calm*) Mr Babcock is downstairs.

TIMOTHY (*excitedly*) Babcock? Not *the* Mr Babcock.

URSULA
BILL } (*together*) Yes, he's here. Yes!

TIMOTHY Babcock, the Hollywood millionaire? The movie magnate? He's considering us as Britain's answer to Fred Astaire and Ginger Rogers. (*He breaks into song.*) "I won't dance, don't ask me – " (*Poses.*)

BILL No we won't.

TIMOTHY Mr Babcock saw us at the Tivoli in The Follies of 1926. (*He goes into another pose.*)

URSULA Mr Babcock is here for the wedding.

TIMOTHY Well he's left it rather late. We were married this morning at St. Barnabas.

URSULA When you say "we" –

TIMOTHY (*interrupting her*) Just a second. You weren't the girl with the Prince of Wales at Tubby Carrington's shoot?

URSULA I don't think so.

TIMOTHY Right. Now as I said in my letter –

BILL Letter?

TIMOTHY When I booked your bridal suite.

BILL Oh, that letter.

TIMOTHY We're just going to be here a couple of days before honeymooning in the South of France. (*To* URSULA.) Although if this weather holds up we might cancel Monte Carlo and honeymoon here.

URSULA Sounds absolutely topping.

TIMOTHY (*to* BILL) So if you could let me see the menu, my little bride and I will have a leisurely lunch on the Terrace.

BILL Very good sir.

POLLY Couldn't we have it sent up to our room, Royston?

TIMOTHY That's an even better idea my little poppet. (*To* BILL.) Will you arrange that?

BILL I didn't quite hear what madam said.

TIMOTHY We'll have lunch sent up to our room.

URSULA Oh will you?

TIMOTHY Just me and my little koochy-coo.

URSULA Well you and your little koochy, can't.

TIMOTHY I beg your pardon?

BILL There's no room service today.

TIMOTHY Playing havoc isn't it, this wretched General Strike. (*To* POLLY.) Well it looks like lunch on the terrace my old banana. (*Then to* BILL.) And then this afternoon we'll take a punt on the river?

BILL River? What river?

TIMOTHY The River Thames.

BILL (*to* URSULA) Thames?

TIMOTHY The Bridal Suite overlooks it.

BILL Oh, does it?

TIMOTHY You mentioned it in your brochure.

BILL (*to* URSULA) Well, I suppose if we mentioned it in our brochure –

TIMOTHY (*to* URSULA) Tell me, have you been on it?

URSULA No, but I'm liable to start any minute now.

(GERALD *dashes in from in the hall.*)

GERALD He won't go away.

TIMOTHY (*to* GERALD) Ah, Porter, there you are. You won't forget to collect those bags and take them up to the bridal suite, will you? (*Hands another £1 coin to* GERALD.)

GERALD (*saluting*) No, sir. Thank you very much, sir.

BILL Where's Babcock?

GERALD Down in the hall. (*Points to* TIM.) Wants to see sir.

TIMOTHY Wants to see me? (*Starts to sing and dance "Top Hat, Putting on my Top Hat".*) I'll see him right away.

URSULA (*stopping him*) No, you won't.

TIMOTHY That's very wise. Mustn't appear too eager.

URSULA (*to* BILL) Bill, take him through there and down into the kitchen.

TIMOTHY The kitchen? Stars of our calibre can't be seen going through the kitchen.

BILL It's the best way to dodge the fans.

(BILL *pushes* TIMOTHY *towards the dining room.*)

TIMOTHY (*suddenly*) By George, I've got it!

BILL Oh God.

TIMOTHY (*to* URSULA) Lady Barrington-Perkins.

URSULA What?

TIMOTHY You're Lady Barrington-Perkins.

URSULA Am I?

BILL Yes!

(*He pushes* TIMOTHY *off.* TIMOTHY *comes straight back for* POLLY *who twirls out through the dining room door.* TIM *follows with a twirl and a leap.*)

GERALD (*very puzzled*) Well, he's done some pretty odd things today, but that takes the biscuit. (*He mimes what he saw, but creaks a bit over the leap.*)

URSULA Bill, go and get a hammer and chisel and get that lock off Judy's door.

BILL I've heard of a shotgun wedding, but this is ridiculous.

(BILL *exits into hall as* TIMOTHY *re-enters from dining room. He gives* GERALD *a £1 tip.*)

TIMOTHY The bags – to the bridal suite, please.

(*He exits into dining room leaving* GERALD *perplexed.*)

GERALD Yes, sir. Thank you very much, sir. (*Holding up the note.*) Could somebody please tell me . . .

URSULA No, they couldn't. Where exactly have you put Mr Babcock?

GERALD Down in the hall, and be won't budge till he's seen Timothy.

URSULA Oh, my God!

GERALD He seems very cross, too. Perhaps Timothy could cheer him up with a couple of little do-dah's. (*Repeats 'jump' business.*)

URSULA No, he couldn't. You hold the fort here with Mr Babcock and I'll help Bill with Judy. I'll get her down here if I have to break every bone in her body.

BABCOCK (*off*) Mr Westerby? Mr Westerby!

URSULA Is that Mr Babcock?

BABCOCK (*off*) Mr Westerby, where the bloody hell are you?

GERALD That's Mr Babcock, yes. (*Puts on his coat.*)

(CHARLES BABCOCK *enters,* U.C. *He is a large bronzed man in his fifties, and speaks with a strong Australian accent. He is wearing a full morning suit, and carrying his top hat. He is barely controlling his temper.*)

BABCOCK I'm looking for Mr Westerby.

URSULA (*gaily*) You must be Mr Babcock. It's Mr Babcock, father. Come along in, Mr Babcock. How do you do – I'm Ursula Westerby.

BABCOCK Oh. I'm very pleased to make your acquaintance. But why the hell aren't you lot down at the Church?

URSULA First things first. (*To* GERALD.) Get Mr Babcock some champagne, father.

GERALD Champagne coming up, sir. (*He goes to open fresh bottle.*)

URSULA (*to* BABCOCK) Isn't it all ripping, absolutely ripping. D'you know, you're just as I pictured you, only younger.

BABCOCK Lady, there is chaos down at that Church.

URSULA (*brightly*) Yes. (*Pushing him towards sofa.*) Do sit down and make yourself at home, only don't forget the cars are here, so you mustn't keep us here chatting.

BABCOCK (*exasperated*) Look, the guests for the *next* damn wedding are starting to arrive.

URSULA And don't worry about Judy. (*Hastily.*) Not that you were – not that you *need* to. She's absolutely er – well thrilled just isn't the word – she's quite overcome, isn't she, father?

GERALD Eh? What's that?

URSULA I said Judy's quite overcome.

GERALD Oh yes. She won't come out.

(URSULA *laughs gaily.*)

URSULA She won't come out and say it. But we know her, we know her very well indeed. Not as well as your Nicholas does of course – (*She suddenly stops on realising what she's said.*) Now you're probably wondering why Judy isn't exactly – er – precisely – completely – one hundred percent ready.

BABCOCK Too bloody right.

URSULA Yes. Everything was running as smooth as clockwork, a little trouble with a hook and eye on the back of the dress, but you know what dresses are like today. It's probably the cotton they use. Now, where was I?

BABCOCK Everything was running smooth as clockwork.

URSULA Until Timothy had this unfortunate accident, which I believe we sort of mentioned to you when you telephoned.

(BABCOCK *nods.*)

GERALD (*cheerfully approaching with Champagne*) In fact you telephoned more than once didn't you sir?

BABCOCK Three bloody times.

GERALD Yes, three bloody times.

URSULA It's such rotten luck for Timothy isn't it? On his daughter's wedding day to break his neck. (BABCOCK *looks incredulous.*) – Leg. He was all ready to leave with Judy, in fact they were just going down the steps when he tripped –

BABCOCK Over a cat called Polly.

GERALD It was a kitten, actually, sir.

BABCOCK (*to* URSULA) And your mother thought it was a blanket.

URSULA Yes.

BABCOCK She also said something about a triple fracture.

URSULA Yes. He broke it in three places. When I say three places, I don't mean that he fell *over* in three places.

(BABCOCK *shakes his head.*)

I mean that he broke it in –

BABCOCK (*interrupting*) Three bloody places.

URSULA Yes.

BABCOCK Mrs Westerby, I want to see your husband.

URSULA (*nervously*) See him?

BABCOCK Yes. I want to know if this wedding is going to take place.

URSULA I'm sure it is.

BABCOCK So what I'd like is five minutes sane conservation with your husband.

URSULA Wouldn't we all.

BABCOCK Come again.

URSULA What I mean is Mr Westerby's gone to St. Thomas's.

BABCOCK St. Thomas's? No wonder. He's at the wrong Church. We're all at St. Barnabas.

URSULA No, no, no, St. Thomas's is a hospital.

BABCOCK Mr Westerby's in hospital?

URSULA (*thinking madly*) Er – I beg your pardon?

BABCOCK I said Mr Westerby's in hospital, is he?

GERALD You talking about Timothy, he was in here just a minute ago.

URSULA Oh, yes of course, he was. How stupid of me. I'd forgotten. (*To* BABCOCK.) But very heavily plastered.

BABCOCK Heavily –

URSULA (*quickly*) Plastered.

GERALD Plastered? Well of course, that explains everything.

BABCOCK Then I can see him.

URSULA See who.

BABCOCK Your husband.

URSULA Er – no. He's upstairs on the bed resting his leg. I'd forgotten.

BABCOCK You don't seem to have a very retentive memory Mrs Westerby.

URSULA Well, it's been one of those days.

BABCOCK Then I'll go up and see him.

URSULA No! I'll bring him down here to you. (*Hesitating.*) And if I take a little time it'll be because I can't find his crutch.

BABCOCK Well find it as soon as you can, because I'm not leaving here until I've seen your husband and the bride.

URSULA (*edges her way to the door*) I'll be two minutes at the most. Er – (*Then brightly.*) You wouldn't like to go on ahead would you, with my father?

BABCOCK No chance.

URSULA No. Jolly good, quite right, let's go together, eh?

BABCOCK Too true.

URSULA Yes, just one big happy family.

(*She laughs gaily and exits.*)

GERALD I don't know what she's got to be so cheerful about, I'm sure. By the way I want to apologise for calling you Babcock, Mr Alcock. I don't know what on earth made me think of it. I mean it's not as if I've ever known anyone called Babcock. Can I give you a small refill?

BABCOCK No. Make it a large one.

GERALD (*gets Champagne*) Large one coming up, sir. I mean it's such a damn silly name isn't it? (*Pours the Champagne.*) Babcock, eh. That reminds me, we had a boy at school called Haddock. We used to call him fish-face. (*He chuckles then stops.*) No I'm wrong that was Salmon. Well, cheers!

BABCOCK (*flatly*) Cheers.

(*They drink.*)

GERALD It's a funny thing about names, Mr Pollock.

(*He sits down beside* MR BABCOCK *and accidently squashes* BABCOCK'S *top hat.* BABCOCK *closes his eyes in anguish, but* GERALD *oblivious of what he's done carries on regardless.*)

It's never been my strong suit, you know. Even when I was in practice I couldn't tell one patient from another. I remember once we had a Mrs Shufflebothom in the surgery. Now you wouldn't think you could forget a name like Shufflebothom, would you? Well, there she was, sitting in the surgery, and I said to her –

BABCOCK Would you mind standing up.

GERALD No, nothing like that, no. What I said was –

BABCOCK (*controlling his rage*) You're sitting on my hat.

GERALD No, I said nothing of the sort. Sitting on my hat indeed. No, what I said was . . . – (*Suddenly.*) Oh. (*Gets up.*) I'm so sorry. I do beg your pardon –

(*He rises and picks up the dented top hat. As he and* BABCOCK *stare at it there is a sound of banging coming from upstairs.*)

BABCOCK What the hell's that?

(DAPHNE *enters.*)

DAPHNE Gerald, you must come at once. I think Ursula's going to kill – (*She suddenly sees* BABCOCK.) Oh! (*Gushingly to* BABCOCK.) You must be Mr Babcock. There's nothing quite like a wedding is there? The sun's singing, the birds are shining – (*Sees the hat in* GERALD's *hand.*) What happened to that?

GERALD I'm afraid I sat on it.

DAPHNE (*angry*) Oh, Gerald, you are a clumsy man. (*She grabs the hat from him.*) Really! (*In an attempt to straighten it out she pushes her hand through the top.*) Now look what you've made me do. Well you'll just have to go without one, that's all.

GERALD It's not mine, it's his.

DAPHNE (*aghast*) Oh!! (*Then sweetly to* BABCOCK.) We'll get you another one right away. (*To* GERALD.) Gerald! (*Loud whisper.*) You've got to help to get that door off its hinges. Hurry!

GERALD (*to* BABCOCK) Remind me to tell you what I said to that woman in the surgery.

DAPHNE What woman?

BABCOCK Mrs Wagglebothom.

GERALD I thought it was Shufflebothom.

DAPHNE Gerald! Will you please come. They're waiting for you. (*She pushes him into the hall. They exit, with* DAPHNE *throwing* BABCOCK *a beaming smile as she closes the doors after them.* BABCOCK, *bewildered, shakes his head, looks at his champagne and decides that strong whisky and soda would be preferable. He goes to pour himself one. His back is to the dining room door as* TIMOTHY *enters.* TIMOTHY, *not seeing* BABCOCK *is looking around for the "Manager". Finally he sees* BABCOCK.)

TIMOTHY Hello there.

(BABCOCK *who is just about to squirt the soda into his whisky is startled and shoots it onto his suit.*)

Sorry about that my old fruit.

BABCOCK That's alright. Just the whole bloody outfit ruined now.

TIMOTHY (*mopping him down*) I really am most frightfully sorry.

BABCOCK It's alright, It's alright.

TIMOTHY Are you stopping here?

BABCOCK No longer than I have to.

TIMOTHY Oh really. You're not happy with the service then?

BABCOCK The Service? I don't think they'll ever get that far. I take it you're a guest here, are you?

TIMOTHY Yes, I've just arrived. I was looking for the staff actually.

BABCOCK You won't find any staff about. The only staff they need here are those big fellers in white coats.

TIMOTHY Well if there's no wine waiter about I'll just have to help myself to a snifter, won't I?

BABCOCK You do that.

(TIMOTHY *pours himself a whisky.*)

TIMOTHY It's this damned General Strike you know.

BABCOCK I knew it was serious. I'd no idea it was general.

TIMOTHY Oh yes. It's all over the country now. It came through on the wireless last night.

BABCOCK On the er – wireless?

TIMOTHY The wireless. I've got one you know.

BABCOCK Have you.

TIMOTHY Oh, yes. It came through just as I was fiddling with the cat's whisker.

BABCOCK That bloody cat gets around.

TIMOTHY I shouldn't worry about it, though, because Mr Baldwin will soon settle it.

BABCOCK Mr Who?

TIMOTHY Stanley Baldwin.

BABCOCK Who the hell's that?

TIMOTHY My dear fellow, he's our Prime Minister.

BABCOCK Is he.

TIMOTHY Yes. Doing a grand job, too. (*Raises glass.*) Stanley Baldwin.

BABCOCK (*raising his glass*) Stanley Baldwin. I've heard of outsiders sneaking up, but where the hell did he come from?

TIMOTHY Oh, he's been around a few years. Cheers.

BABCOCK Cheers.

TIMOTHY Mind you, I think the country would be well advised to recall Lloyd George.

(BACOCK *tries to work this out.*)

BABCOCK (*flatly*) You do.

TIMOTHY Yes. He's the fellow for the gun-boat diplomacy. You haven't heard a lot from the Kaiser lately, have you?

BABCOCK (*pause*) Could I have a drop more soda in this, please?

TIMOTHY (*bringing the syphon to him*) Certainly. If there's no-one around, we'll just have to fend for ourselves, won't we Mr er –

BABCOCK Babcock.

TIMOTHY Babcock!?

(*He inadvertantly squirts the soda fiercely into* BABCOCK'S *glass, thereby soaking him.*)

BABCOCK (*outraged*) What are you doing?

TIMOTHY I say I do apologise. (*Mopping him down.*) I really do.

BABCOCK (*grabs the handkerchief*) It's alright. I'll do it.

TIMOTHY You are really *the* Mr Babcock?

BABCOCK Yes, I am and I'm beginning to wish I wasn't.

TIMOTHY This is absolutely spiffing. (*Squirts soda again.*)

BABCOCK (*backing away*) Will you please put that thing down

(TIMOTHY *puts the syphon down.*)

TIMOTHY Don't you remember me Mr Babcock?

BABCOCK I can't say I do.

TIMOTHY The Follies.

BABCOCK The what?

TIMOTHY Would you like to see my "Black Bottom"?

BABCOCK I beg your pardon?

(TIMOTHY *decides to jog his memory by going into the first few bars, dancing and singing "The Black Bottom".* BABCOCK *takes a step towards the door.*)

TIMOTHY (*stopping*) There we are.

BABCOCK Thanks, very nice.

TIMOTHY You still don't remember, do you?

BABCOCK Not quite, no. If you'll excuse me I think I'll just go and have a word –

TIMOTHY (*stopping him*) Tivoli!

BABCOCK Pardon?

TIMOTHY You saw me at the Tivoli. You must recognise me.

BABCOCK I'd like to oblige, but no.

TIMOTHY Of course I'm not wearing my make-up now.

BABCOCK Very wise.

(BABCOCK *is now looking for some means of escape.*)

TIMOTHY Mr Babcock. I am your answer to Fred! (*Pose.*)

BABCOCK Fred?

TIMOTHY And I want to show you my little koochy-koo. (*Pose.*)

BABCOCK No, thanks.

TIMOTHY I've got somebody in there who could be another Ginger.

BABCOCK Thanks for telling me.

TIMOTHY (*opens dining room door*) In you come my little sweetheart.

(POLLY *enters and dances around* MR BABCOCK *who of course can't see her. She sings "I Want To Be Happy".*)

What d'you think of her?

BABCOCK (*looking round*) Who? (POLLY *goes into tap dance.*)

TIMOTHY (*pointing to her feet*) The other half of my act.

BABCOCK (*looking on the floor*) What is she, a performing flea?

TIMOTHY (*laughing*) Now stop your kidding, Mr Babcock. Just look at that potential. I mean what's Ginger got that this girl hasn't?

BABCOCK (*backing towards the hall door*) I've no idea.

(POLLY *stops dancing and singing.* TIMOTHY *applauds her.*)

TIMOTHY Lovely, my darling. (*To* BABCOCK.) Hey, where are you going?

BABCOCK I'm already late for a very important engagement.

TIMOTHY You haven't seen what we can do together yet.

BABCOCK I'd rather not, thanks.

TIMOTHY We've got the best finish in the business.

BABCOCK Bully for you.

(TIMOTHY *and* POLLY *go into a song and dance routine of "Over My Shoulder".* BABCOCK *attempts to tip-toe out of the room but* URSULA *enters.*)

URSULA (*brightly*) Here we are, nearly ready. Judy won't be long. (*To* TIMOTHY.) What are you doing in here?

TIMOTHY (*still dancing*) Auditioning for Mr Babcock.

URSULA (*laughs gaily*) Oh, lovely. (*To* BABCOCK.) Isn't that lovely.

(*Apprehensively to* TIM.) And Polly?

TIMOTHY Yes, she's right here.

URSULA Super-dooper.

BABCOCK Who is this nut?

URSULA (*pauses – then firmly*) I don't know.

TIMOTHY (*to* URSULA) It's because I'm not wearing make-up that he doesn't recognise me. (*Then proudly to* BABCOCK.) Royston Westerby.

BABCOCK Westerby? You mean this character's a relative?

TIMOTHY And this my new bride, Polly Perkins. (*He and* POLLY *start to sing and dance "Heaven, I'm in Heaven".*)

BABCOCK I thought you said you didn't know him.

URSULA I didn't know he was here. He's a cousin.

BABCOCK Cousin?

URSULA Of my husband's.

BABCOCK Good God Almighty!

URSULA Oh, it's alright. Twice removed.

(TIM *and* POLLY *continue dancing for* BABCOCK'S *benefit.*)

BABCOCK And third time coming up.

URSULA He's fairly harmless. We don't see a lot of him normally.

BABCOCK I can well believe it. Where's he from.

URSULA Basingstoke.

BABCOCK Basingstoke?

URSULA Hants.

BABCOCK Come again.

URSULA Short for Hampshire.

BABCOCK Had a case like this last year in Queensland.

URSULA Oh, really?

BABCOCK They put it down to drinking sheep-dip.

(TIMOTHY *and* POLLY *dance to* C., then she goes L. *and* TIMOTHY *does a solo,* C.)

Do you have many sheep in Basingstoke?

URSULA Not a lot, no.

BABCOCK (*watching* TIM) Well, he's getting it from somewhere.

(TIMOTHY *unsuccessfully attempts the "splits".*)

That'll make his eyes water.

TIMOTHY (*pointing towards* POLLY) Isn't she absolutely adorable, Mr Babcock? (*He dives and lands on the sofa, then rises to follow* POLLY *as she flits away again.*)

BABCOCK (*moving to where* POLLY *was a moment ago*) And what about this female midget of his?

URSULA Female what?

BABCOCK The one he's supposed to be dancing with – answers to Ginger.

URSULA Oh, he's told you about her, has he?

BABCOCK I hope Cousin Royston's trouble doesn't run through the family.

URSULA Oh, good heavens, no. And my side of the family's as sound as a bell.

(GERALD *pops his head in from the hall.*)

GERALD We're all unhinged now.

URSULA Jolly good. (*To* BABCOCK.) The door, a little trouble with the door.

BABCOCK So I believe.

(TIMOTHY *and* POLLY *have stopped dancing.*)

TIMOTHY What about that contract, Mr Babcock.

BABCOCK Contract?

TIMOTHY For your new Hollywood musical.

URSULA Please, some other time.

BABCOCK Yes, some other bloody time.

POLLY Oh, language.

TIMOTHY Just a slip of the tongue, Polly.

BABCOCK I could cheerfully drown that damn Polly.

TIMOTHY (*to* POLLY) You'd better wait outside, while I talk terms.

POLLY Righty-oh Royston. Goodbye-ee! (*She flits away.*)

TIMOTHY Off you go. Godbyeeee!

POLLY Goodbyeeee!

(*She exits into the hall.* TIMOTHY *waves her off.*)

GERALD There goes the twelve-ten.

(JUDY *enters with* DAPHNE.)

DAPHNE Grannie's sorted it all out, and our little bride's all ready for the car.

TIMOTHY (*to* JUDY) Good Lord, what a coincidence. I was married only this morning.

JUDY You what?

URSULA (*trying to intervene*) One moment Royston.

TIMOTHY (*to* JUDY) Yes, Royston Westerby. (*Shakes her hand.*) I'm delighted to make your acquaintance. I'll ask the porter to take your bags up.

(*She bursts into tears and rushes off.*)

BABCOCK Was that the bride?

URSULA Yes that's my little Judy.

TIMOTHY Good heaven's, I didn't know you were the bride's mother, Lady Barrington?

BABCOCK Lady Barrington!

URSULA My maiden name, I dropped the title when I married.

(DAPHNE *who has been unable to comprehend anything since she's been in the room, suddenly lets out a wail and stamps her feet like a bad-tempered child.*)

DAPHNE Ahh! !

GERALD What is it old girl, your corset?

DAPHNE (*sobbing*) Ahh! !

BABCOCK Bloody 'ell.

URSULA Mother please, pull yourself together.

(DAHPNE *whimpers.*)

GERALD It could be pinching. I'll take her upstairs and strip her down.

TIMOTHY (*to* URSULA) I think I'd better go along in case the porter gets too familiar.

DAPHNE Ahh! !

(DAPHNE, GERALD *and* TIMOTHY *exit.*)

BABCOCK Jeez.

URSULA I do hope Mrs Babcock won't be getting worried about you, Mr Babcock.

BABCOCK Never mind about Mrs Babcock, *I'm* getting worried about me.

URSULA Yes. We're all so looking forward to meeting her.

BABCOCK There's only one person I want to meet and that's Mr Westerby.

URSULA Yes.

BABCOCK And I don't mean dippy Cousin Royston.

URSULA No.

BABCOCK So regardless of his crutch and his plaster I'll go up and see him.

URSULA I'd much, much rather you didn't.

BABCOCK Listen, unless I speak to your husband, and right now, I'm calling the whole thing off.

URSULA Oh you wouldn't do that.

BABCOCK Yes I would, and will. I'm not having my son marry into a family of raving lunatics. There's got to be one sane person in this house and it had better be your husband.

(BILL *enters.*)

BILL Don't worry, Ursula, I think everything's going to be alright Judy's . . .

URSULA (*interrupts*) Talk of the devil.

BILL (*blankly*) Huh?

URSULA Hullo, darling. (*Gives him a big kiss and takes his arm.*)

BILL (*confused*) Oh, hello. (URSULA *points at* BABCOCK, *mouthing his name.*) You must be Mr Babcock. (*Goes to shake hands.*)

BABCOCK Yes, and am I pleased to meet you.

BILL Likewise.

BABCOCK Where's your crutch?

BILL (*pause*) I beg your pardon? (*Embarrassed, he edges away.*)

BABCOCK I thought you were plastered.

(BILL *looks blankly at* URSULA.)

URSULA So did I Mr Babcock. That's so like him though. Determined to press on in the face of all adversity. That's my *Timothy.*

BILL Huh?

URSULA That's my husband, Timothy Westerby.

(*Hugs his arm.*)

BILL Would you mind If I go out and come in again. (*Moving towards hall.*)

BABCOCK That's a good idea. Keep moving about on it.

BILL On what?

URSULA Your fracture.

BILL (*returning*) Oh on that (*Shakes, then slaps leg.*) That seems to have done the trick.

BABCOCK You take a triple fracture very lightly Mr Westerby, or do I call you Tim?

BILL Well er – (*To* URSULA.) Does he?

URSULA (*firmly*) Yes, he does.

BABCOCK Now look I've just got one question to ask you and you'd better make more sense than your cousin did.

BILL Cousin?

URSULA He's met your dippy cousin Royston.

BABCOCK Oh. Is that good?

BABCOCK Didn't you know he was here?

BILL No.

BABCOCK Escaped, I knew it.

BILL (*to* URSULA) Just let me get one thing absolutely straight. When you say my dippy cousin is here –

URSULA I mean Royston and *Polly*.

BILL Oh, that dippy cousin.

BABCOCK How many dippy cousins have you got?

BILL Only Royston. He's just a little eccentric, that's all.

BABCOCK Well I want to know what you and your daughter intend to do.

BILL Me and my daughter?

URSULA That's Judy.

BILL I know who my daughter is.

BABCOCK You're already fifteen minutes late. Now are you coming or do me and my lady wife take the first plane back to Sydney.

URSULA We wouldn't like them to do that darling, would we, darling.

BILL No darling. We wouldn't darling.

(JUDY *enters with* DAPHNE *and* GERALD.)

DAPHNE Ursula, the drivers want to know if there's any point in waiting.

URSULA Well, of course there is. Are you and Judy alright now?

DAPHNE Yes we're fine. Gerald gave us some of his medicine. Very settling.

BABCOCK Hullo Judy. I just hope you'll stay around this time long enough for me to introduce myself.

JUDY Yes, I'm sorry about that Mr Babcock, I'm fine now.

BABCOCK Good. Good. I can see now why my Nicholas gave the brush to all those Sheila's back home.

JUDY Thank you.

BABCOCK So let's all get to the Church now shall we?

URSULA Good idea. You go on ahead.

BABCOCK Oh no. I'm going to make sure Judy and Father are locked safely in that car.

JUDY You mean Daddy's coming?

BABCOCK Yes, he's made a remarkable recovery.

JUDY Oh marvellous.

DAPHNE Well, that's a relief.

JUDY You know, that's one of the reasons I was so miserable.

URSULA Of course it is darling. Now, shall you and I go down together?

BABCOCK No, no Judy goes with her Dad.

URSULA I think it would be wiser if she went with me.

BILL I second that.

DAPHNE What are you talking about, Ursula, the bride always goes with her father.

BABCOCK Too true. (*To* BILL.) Mr Westerby, take your daughter's . . .

(*He thrusts* JUDY'S *arm through* BILL'S. JUDY *looks at* BILL *who tries to put on a comforting smile.*)

There we are. Thank God, at last. Like you said, Mrs Westerby, just one big happy family.

(JUDY'S *face crumbles and she starts to cry and rushes off.*)

URSULA Judy!

BABCOCK Now what?

URSULA She's so happy.

DAPHNE (*puzzled*) I think I'm a little in the dark.

BILL Don't worry, you're in very good company.

(*From offstage* TIMOTHY *is heard calling out.*)

TIMOTHY (*off*) Polly? Polly?

BABCOCK Hell, it's dippy Royston again. Get him out of here.

(TIMOTHY *enters from the hall with* POLLY. *They are singing and dancing, "My Blue Heaven".* BABCOCK *despairs and sits down while* BILL *and* URSULA *try to placate him with a drink.)*

TIMOTHY "A turn to the right, a little white light, will lead you to my blue heaven".

GERALD Hey, I know that thing. (*He starts to sing and dance with* TIMOTHY.) "You'll see a smiling face, a fireplace, a cosy room".

TIMOTHY
POLLY
GERALD (*together*) "A little nest that nestles where the roses bloom"

TIMOTHY "Just Polly and me"

GERALD Er-two, er-three, "And Daphne makes three"

TIMOTHY
POLLY
GERALD (*together*)
"We're happy in my blue heaven"
(*Finale Pose.*)

GERALD Hot dog! They don't write them like that any more.

DAPHNE Sit down, Gerald!

GERALD Shut up, Daphne.

(DAPHNE *collapses in astonishment.*)

BILL Anyone care for a drink?

(TIMOTHY *and* POLLY *start to sing and dance "California, Here I Come" concurrently with the following dialogue.*)

TIMOTHY & POLLY California, here I come . . .

BABCOCK I'm going to phone the Church.

URSULA What on earth for?

BABCOCK To tell my Nicholas to clear off before it's too late.

DAPHNE Try and look on the bright side, Mr Babcock.

BABCOCK The bright side?

DAPHNE Yes, the bright side!

TIMOTHY Big finish coming up, Mr Babcock!

BABCOCK I'm calling this wedding off *now.*

DAPHNE You can't – we've got 400 guests waiting at the Church.

BABCOCK I should worry. They're probably as loopy as you lot.

T & P: back where I started from ... Where bowers have flowers That bloom in spring At dawning, each morning Birdies sing and everything ... A sun-kissed miss said 'Don't be late', That's why I can hardly wait, Open up that Golden Gate, California ... here I come! (POLLY *dances off, and* TIMOTHY *returns.*)

TIMOTHY (*singing*) Oh, open up that Golden Gate ...

(*To* URSULA.) Lady Barrington ...

(*To* BABCOCK.) Mr Babcock ...

(*To* BILL.) Hotel Manager ...

(*To* GERALD.) Stanley Baldwin ...

(*To* DAPHNE.) Mrs Pankhurst ...

California ... here I come!

(*He goes to make an impressive exit and accidently dives out through the open window onto the marquee below, which collapses. Crashing sounds, canvas tearing, crockery and glass smashing, people shouting and general noise of chaos float up. There is a stunned silence for a second or two and everyone rushes to see what's happened. Everyone, that is, except* BABCOCK *who sits and cries.*)

DAPHNE He jumped out of the window. He's ruined that marquee.

BILL It broke his fall though.

(BABCOCK *cries loudly.*)

URSULA Go and see if he's alright, and I'll phone for a doctor.

(BILL *rushes off.*)

DAPHNE Timothy! Are you alright? Timothy! (*She rushes off.*)

URSULA (*angrily*) Pull yourself together Mr Babcock.

GERALD (*laughs*) Oh, that was very good, but I still think the best of the lot is the little do-dah.

(GERALD *exits doing the "stepping over nothing" business.* URSULA *is dialling a phone number.)*

BABCOCK (*tearfully*) It's a bad dream. Tell me it's a bad dream.

(TIMOTHY *enters from the dining room, with glass of champagne. He is bright, cheerful, confident and completely cured. Jaunty in grey topper.*)

URSULA Darling are you alright?

TIMOTHY Yes I'm fine. I've just been talking to that Catering Manager and he seems to think we're behind schedule. (*Takes off topper.*)

(URSULA *puts down phone.*)

URSULA Now just you go and lie down, Cousin Royston.

(*Throughout the ensuring few lines it dawns on* URSULA *that* TIMOTHY *is back to normal.*)

TIMOTHY I beg your pardon?

BABCOCK Lady Barrington said lie down Cousin Royston.

TIMOTHY Lady who?

BABCOCK Barrington.

TIMOTHY (*referring to* BABCOCK) Who's this?

BABCOCK Or better still go back to Basingstoke.

TIMOTHY Basingstoke?

BABCOCK Hants!

TIMOTHY Huh?

BABCOCK Hants, short for Hampshire.

TIMOTHY (*to* BABCOCK) Are you with the caterers? (BABCOCK *bursts into tears again.*) What's the matter, has someone trodden on the cake? (BABCOCK *continues to weep. To* URSULA.) Well come on, darling. We ought to get a move on. or Mr Babcock will think there's a hitch. (BABCOCK *sobs again.*)

URSULA (*to* TIMOTHY) Just a minute. I do believe you're normal.

BABCOCK Normal! (*Wails.*)

TIMOTHY Have we given him a dud cheque or something?

URSULA S'your Polly gone?

TIMOTHY Polygon? What's that?

URSULA She is. That's marvellous.

TIMOTHY I think today's been too much for you.

BABCOCK Too much for her?! (*Wails.*)

TIMOTHY I've heard of crying at weddings but this is ridiculous. I mean, he's with the caterers. Go and do some work in the garden! The bloody tent's fallen down!

URSULA (*urgently to* TIMOTHY) That's Mr "B".

TIMOTHY (*to* BABCOCK) Mr Barrington! Mr Barrington of Perkins Bras. (*Shakes him warmly by the hand.*) Hello, I'm sorry I didn't pick you up this morning.

BABCOCK Keep your distance.

TIMOTHY Everything's under control.

BABCOCK Good, good.

TIMOTHY I've got the perfect answer to your bra problem.

BABCOCK My what?

TIMOTHY Perkins can take the flop out of flappers.

BABCOCK Mrs Westerby, isn't it time for his pill or something.

URSULA Yes, it is.

TIMOTHY No. I don't want a pill. I don't want a pill ever again. I feel a different person.

BABCOCK I think that's your trouble.

TIMOTHY The Perkins girl will be on the buses, underground, up and down the escalators –

BABCOCK Sounds exhausting.

URSULA I really don't think *Mr Babcock's* interested dear.

TIMOTHY 'Course he is, your bra will go round the world.

URSULA Mr *Babcock* is nothing to do with bras.

TIMOTHY I know that. I'm talking about Mr Barring . . .

URSULA (*pointing and mouthing*) Mr Babcock –

TIMOTHY (*realising*) Mr Babcock! (*Puts arm round him.*) Good heavens. You're soaking wet, Mr Babcock. Did you swim from Australia? Are you really Mr Babcock?

BABCOCK God only knows who I am. (*Sits.*)

TIMOTHY (*shaking him warmly by the hand*) Mr Babcock, how do you do, I'm so happy to meet you at last. I really am. (*Laughs.*) You must think me a bit of an idiot.

BABCOCK (*to* URSULA) Does he expect an answer?

TIMOTHY (*soothingly*) I know why you're so upset, you know.

BABCOCK You do?

TIMOTHY Oh, yes, I do. Nicholas is your only child. You've come all this way and you find yourself surrounded by strange people.

URSULA Mr Babcock isn't feeling that.

BABCOCK He bloody well is.

TIMOTHY But, look at it this way – you're not losing a son, you're gaining a whole family.

(BABCOCK *wails and rushes away to sit with his head in his hands away from* TIMOTHY. BILL *enters with* GERALD *following.*)

BILL It's the most extraordinary thing. We can't find him any – Oh, there you are. You ought to be in bed.

TIMOTHY In bed?

BILL (*points to* GERALD) The porter will take you up.

(GERALD *holds out his hand for the by now customary tip.*)

GERALD Yes, sir, thank you, sir.

(TIMOTHY *looks at* GERALD, *uncomprehending.*)

BILL Go on, up you go.

BABCOCK Yes. And take Polly, Fred and Ginger with you.

(TIMOTHY *looks at* BABCOCK.)

TIMOTHY (*puzzled*) Polly, Fred and Ginger?

BILL (*cutting in*) I'll explain later. Get upstairs now.

TIMOTHY But I've got to get to –

BILL Listen, as long as I'm Manager of this hotel I give the orders.

TIMOTHY Hotel?

(TIMOTHY *looks at* URSULA.)

URSULA Let's sort it out after the Ceremony.

BABCOCK No Mrs Westerby, I don't know how I got involved in this madhouse but if I'm going to be driven round the bend, I want to know the exact route I was taken.

GERALD Don't you worry.

BABCOCK Don't worry?

GERALD Leave it to the drivers, they know the way.

BABCOCK I'm going to get an explanation if it kills me.

URSULA Oh, I can explain.

BABCOCK Lady, I'm up to here with your explanations. So would you mind keeping quiet for a minute.

URSULA Yes, it's just that I'm a bit –

BABCOCK Please! I want to talk to your husband.

BABCOCK Please! I want to talk to your husband.

TIMOTHY } (*stepping forward together*) Go ahead.
BILL } Good idea.

BABCOCK (*angrily to* TIMOTHY) I don't want to talk to you, I want to discuss it with him.

TIMOTHY Yes, but's he's Shorter.

BABCOCK What the hell's his height got to do with it?

TIMOTHY (*laughs*) What the hell's his height got to do with it! Very funny, I like that.

BABCOCK Will someone get dippy Cousin Royston out of here.

TIMOTHY Who's dippy Cousin Royston?

BABCOCK Go to Basingstoke!

TIMOTHY Why does he keep saying Basingstoke?

GERALD Ah, Mr Basingstoke, I thought you were Babcock.

(*Shakes hands with* BABCOCK.)

TIMOTHY Look, I'm sorry to break this up. You get into the first car and I'll follow with the bride. Gerald, you go and round up Daphne.

GERALD Alright, but I don't want to miss anything. Let me know if you're going to jump off the roof, won't you. (GERALD *exits.*)

TIMOTHY (*to* BABCOCK) You'll have to forgive Gerald, he's a bit eccentric.

BABCOCK *He's* eccentric?

BILL (*to* TIMOTHY) Hey wait a minute. I do believe you're normal.

BABCOCK S'truth.

TIMOTHY Of course I'm normal. I've never felt better in the whole of my life. I'm on top of the world. Somehow or other I've been set free.

BABCOCK I knew it.

TIMOTHY And why shouldn't I? I've got everything a man could wish for, especially you my darling.

(*He gives* URSULA *a big kiss.* BABCOCK *looks at* BILL.)

BILL We're a very close family.

TIMOTHY (*to* URSULA) And it won't only be the youngsters who are honeymooning tonight. (*Gives her another kiss.*)

BABCOCK (*to* BILL) I tell you, infidelity in Sydney is in its infancy.

BILL I think Mr Babcock ought to be told.

BABCOCK Told what?

URSULA After the wedding, Bill.

BABCOCK Look, if I'm to be told anything, I want to be – (*Stops.*) Just a minute – you called him Bill.

URSULA That's right.

BILL I am Bill.

BABCOCK I thought your husband's name was Tim.

TIMOTHY It is.

BABCOCK Will you be quiet. (*To* BILL.) Is your name Tim Westerby or Bill Westerby.

BILL Neither.

BABCOCK (*floored*) What?

TIMOTHY I told you he's Shorter.

BABCOCK Shut up!

URSULA Charles dear, I'm very pleased to be able to tell you now that this – (*Indicating* TIMOTHY.) is my husband.

BABCOCK (*slowly looks at* TIMOTHY) You're married to dippy Cousin Royston?

URSULA Yes.

TIMOTHY Who's dippy Cousin Roys–

BILL (*hastily*) I'll explain later.

URSULA Right, off we go, after you Charles (*Tries to usher him out.*)

BABCOCK Oh no! It was bad enough when I thought you were married to him. (*Points to* BILL.) But I'm not having my grandchildren turning out like this nut. (*Points to* TIMOTHY.)

TIMOTHY Nut?

BABCOCK Yes, nut. I'm calling this whole thing off. I'm going to grab my boy Nicholas out of that Church right now.

URSULA Charles, please. (*Restrains him.*)

(*The telephone rings.* BILL *picks up the receiver.*)

BILL (*into phone*) 0343 . . . . . . (*Then to* BABCOCK.) It's for you Mr Babcock. It's your son Nicholas.

BABCOCK (*rushing to phone*) Give me that phone! (*Into phone.*) Nicholas, this is your father here. Don't ask any questions, just grab your mother, tip the Vicar, and slide out of the side door . . . . You've already left the Church? (*To the others.*) He's no fool. (*Back to phone.*) Good on you Nick, you pulled out just in time. Is your mother with you? . . . Just Judy. Judy who? . . . Westerby?!

URSULA Judy?

TIMOTHY Where are they? She's supposed to be going with me to the Church.

BABCOCK Well she's gone with Nicholas to the where? . . . The Fulham Registry Office.

URSULA You mean they're eloping?

BABCOCK Yes. (*Into phone.*) I'll be right over. (*Slams down the phone and turns to* TIMOTHY.) And I only hope I get there before they get to the bit about "any just cause or impediment"! (*He exits.*)

BILL I'm not sorry I've lost him for an in-law.

TIMOTHY Bill, be a pal, go and see the Vicar and the congregation and tell them there's been a slight hitch.

BILL Oh, thank you. What'll I do then? March all 400 of them through Kensington to the Fulham Registry Office?

TIMOTHY No, bring them back here and give them a drink. Just stall them for half an hour.

BILL Oh, great. I'll give them the choice of community singing or a quick knees-up in the Cemetry! (BILL *exits.*)

TIMOTHY How about a drink.

URSULA (*getting her hat and his Topper*) We haven't time now, we've got to rush over to Fulham then drive back here and –

TIMOTHY Relax. (*He kisses her neck.*) If you carry on like that you'll give yourself a nervous breakdown.

(*He kisses her ear, and takes his Topper.*)

URSULA But your daughter's getting married.

TIMOTHY No rush. (*He kisses her cheek.*)

URSULA Aren't you worried about your speech.

TIMOTHY I'm not worried about anything anymore. (*He kisses her mouth.*)

URSULA (*dazed*) Oh, darling.

TIMOTHY What?

URSULA I've gone all wobbly.

TIMOTHY — You better have another one. (*He kisses her again and after a moment she breaks it.*)

URSULA — Hey, it's all this practice you've been having with Polly.

TIMOTHY — Polly?

URSULA — (*smiling*) I'll tell you about her in bed tonight.

(URSULA *kisses him.* GERALD *and* DAPHNE *enter.* GERALD *sports his grey Topper.*)

DAPHNE — Ursula .... (*Stops on seeing them kissing.*) Now what are they doing?

GERALD — Come off it Daphne, your memory can't be that bad.

DAPHNE — (*moving down to* URSULA) Ursula, could we please go to the Church now.

TIMOTHY — No, there's been a slight change of plan. It's the Fulham Registry Office.

DAPHNE — What?

URSULA — That's where they're getting married.

DAPHNE — Gerald and I certainly aren't going to any Registry Office.

GERALD — (*by her side*) We'll have to.

DAPHNE — We are going to the Church.

GERALD — But the Bride and Groom won't be there.

DAPHNE — I don't care. I bought this outfit for St. Barnabas and St. Barnabas's bloody well going to see it! (GERALD *and* DAPHNE *exit.*)

(URSULA *and* TIMOTHY *laugh, kiss, exchange hats and go, arms around each other, to follow them off.*)

THE CURTAIN FALLS.

"THERE GOES THE BRIDE"

FURNITURE AND PROPERTY PLOT

SET ONSTAGE

ACT 1

D.R. Door, opening on, hinged upstage.
Onstage of door, padded stool (matching armchair and sofa.)

R. *to* U.R. Two pairs of long casement windows, side by side. Floor length curtains drawn to upstage and downstage ends, with floor-length net curtain drawn to between the two pairs of windows and net curtain drawn to upstage end of upstage pair of windows.

Downstage set of windows wide open upstage window of upstage pair of windows closed; downstage window of upstage pair of windows, ajar.

U.R. Lamp, on pedestal. On wall: Modern picture in chrome frame Table, with draped damask table cloth, decorated with swagged garlands of tiny pink roses across the front and sides just below table-top level.

ON TABLE Upstage on each end, Champagne bucket. In Stage R. bucket, an opened bottle of champagne. Between the buckets, in a double row, 16 champagne glasses, set rims down.

L. *to* R., below buckets and glasses: Clean folded table napkin; Dish of nuts, dish of twiglets, round glass ashtray, and table lighter.

U.R.C. Round polished antique table. On it: Half-full decanter of whisky, with 6 'tot' glasses round it in semi-circle; Square frosted glass tumbler (for cigarettes).

The above all set to extreme R. of table.

R.C. (below table) Armchair (modern design and upholstery) [Block-board under removable seat cushion to prevent sinking.]

U.C. (flanking double, on-stage opening doors) Small round tables with wrought-iron legs, with two tiers on top, painted white. On bottom tier, white bowls of pink and yellow roses; on 2nd tier, white bowls containing a white blossom with leaves; and on top tier, a single tall vase of yellow roses.

Offstage, in hall – centre, a writing table. On it: white bowl of red roses, right, a mahogany chair; [two small ashtrays left of writing table, a mahogany chair.]

On walls: (over writing table) 4 framed pictures of birds; (over mahogany chair L. of Wr. Table) Red and white floral picture.

Onstage, U.L. Table, draped damask tablecloth, decorated with swagged garlands as U.R.

ON TABLE: Upstage on each end, Champagne bucket. Between the buckets, in double row, 14 champagne glasses, 10 set with rims down, the 4 next to the stage L. bucket right way up L. to R., below buckets and glasses: Clean folded table napkin (fresh each show); dish of cheese (cocktail) biscuits; pair of wire cutters; dish of nuts.

On wall, over table, modern picture in chrome frame (twin to one U.R.).

L. Door to dining-room, hinged upstage, opening on.

In recess above dining room door: oval polished table.

On it; Upstage – Lamp.

Downstage – Vase of roses (yellow).

Centre (onstage) – Glass dish, chocolates and fondants etc.

On wall, over table, Pair gilt wall brackets with silk half-shades Under brackets: A gold-framed picture of sailing ships.

In recess below dining-room door: Drinks table.

On it: Upstage – Vase of yellow roses. Small decanter of whisky.

Centre: – Small silver ice bucket with lid. Bottle of Campari.

D/stage – Half-bottle whisky and "Sparklets" syphon (in front of above) Upstage: 5 stemmed glasses D/stage: 4 Tumblers.

(behind tumblers) Half-bottle brandy; ½-full Jug of Water.

On wall over table: Pair gilt wall brackets with silk half-shades Gold framed picture of a sailing ship.

D.L.C. Large sofa (matching armchair and stool) [Blockboard under 3 removable set cushions to prevent sinking. Arms reinforced, as sat on.]

Behind it, long sofa table.

ON IT, L. *to* R.: Table ashtray, and lighter. Above them, round beribboned box of chocolates and fondants.

3 glass dishes (for sweets).

Black cigarette box (dressing).

Below cig. box, two white ornaments of Swans (for cigs). Index of phone numbers; on top of it, gold box of 200 cigs. Telephone.

OFFSTAGE:

Backing of D.R. door, decorated by two gold framed pictures of sailing ships.

Backing of L. door, decorated by a gilt pair of candelabra with half-shades mounted over an oval gilt-framed mirror.

Outside R. casement windows, red and white striped marquee roof, attached at upstage end to "roof supports" and at downstage end to the wall of theatre by a rope (threaded through the top hem of marquee).

Where the rope emerges from the hem at the downstage end of marquee cloth, a "breaking" mechanism, consisting of the "stirrup" end of a metal shackle, with scenery-pin and 3 wood cocktail sticks, is inserted.

PROPERTIES SET OFFSTAGE

ACT I:

Off D.R. Sewing basket with suitable dressing. On padded lid: Small pair scissors and a needle. Reel of white Silko in basket.

ACT II

Off D.L. Timothy's top hat. Champagne glass.

ACT I:

Off U.L. Box of wedding flowers, containing two bridesmaid's posies, an orchid spray with pin, a carnation spray, 6 various carnations, roses and white blossom as dressing, and a 'trick' rose which collapses.

A 3-ply board 'cut-out' of "Polly Perkins".

An opened bottle, of champagne, and tiny piece Melba toast with 'caviar' on it, Daphne's handbag and gloves, plus non-collapsible matching rose with pin.

Pair white flannels, "Velcro'd" from backwaist to front waist (so they can be torn apart).

Pair of bright, diamond-patterned golfing socks.

Tim's morning suit: Black tail-coat, grey striped trousers, grey waistcoat and grey, black and white silk tie. In R. hand pocket of waistcoat, three new £1 coins. Clean white hanky in tail-coat's breast pocket.

Handbag, hat and gloves—Ursula.

Bride's beribboned posy.

OFF U.L. (*for ACT II*)

Unopened bottle champagne
'trick' top-hat (Babcock)

Hammer or mallet for Knocking effect

Top-hat (Gerald)

PERSONAL PROPS:

Feather Boa-Polly
"Carmen" hair rollers – Judy. Stiff wing collar – Gerald
Wristwatch – Ursula
Wristwatch – Daphne
Unfinished speech and bottles of 'pills' (Amplex capsules) – Tim
Red carnation – Bill
Fob-watch and white carnation – Gerald
White hanky in breast pocket and white carnation in lapel – Babcock

PROP STANDBY'S – offstage

Approx. 19 mins after Curtain Up on Act I: STANDBY D.R. to catch white flannels
Approx. 8 mins after Curtain Up on Act II: STANDBY U.L. for knocking effect

INTERVAL (approx. 60 mins after Curtain Up on Act I)

FROM *Table* U.R., Table behind sofa and Drinks table D.L. remove and wash all dirty glasses, also those on offstage U.L. prop table.

STRIKE: Cut-out behind sofa table to offstage U.L.

SET: Opened champagne bottle from sofa table to Stage L. end of Caterers decorated table U.L.

From prop table off U.L.: Full (unopened) champagne bottle to Stage L. end of Caterers decorated table U.L.

Empty champagne glass off D.L. half full of champagne Clean glasses to original positions on Caterers table U.L. and drinks table D.L., EXCEPT THAT ONLY 4 STEMMED GLASSES ARE RE-SET. SPARE ONE GOES ON OFF U.L. prop table.

Brandy bottle moved to rear of Drinks table D.L., with water jug below it. Whisky bottle moves to position occupied by Brandy bottle, and a Sparklets syphon (now charged with water and sparklets bulb) moves to position occupied by water jug.

RETURN clothes etc. from Tim's Act I change to his room.

REMOVE steel pin from marquee rig D.R. (Orange sticks only linking the shackle to the rope now. When Tim jumps out window onto marquee, the sticks break, and canvas drops onto mattresses etc. underneath).

CHECK: Both downstage windows D.R. wide open. Glasses and bottles re-set.

Babcock's topper offstage U.L. also Judy's bouquet.

Enough room below phone on table for Babcock's hat; if not, move phone upstage to allow for this.

Half-full champagne bottle in bucket on U.R. Caterers table. Syphon spout facing downstage.

Clean folded napkin by champagne bottles on Caterers table U.L.

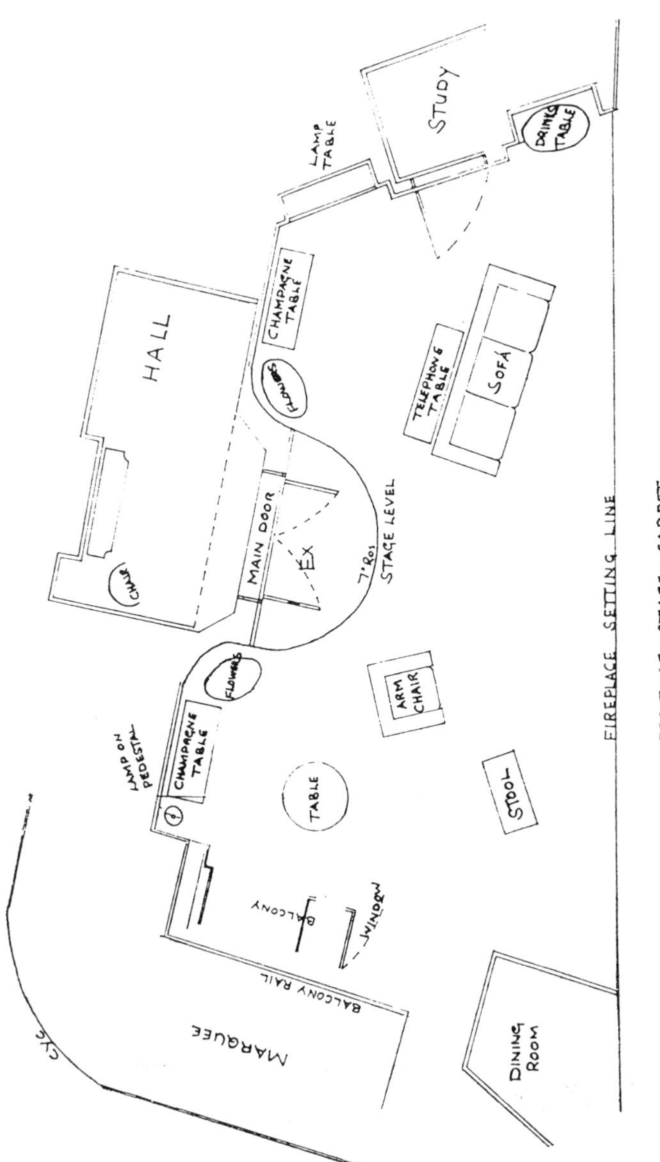
STUDY
LAMP TABLE
DRINKS TABLE
HALL
CHAMPAGNE TABLE
FLOWERS
TELEPHONE TABLE
SOFA
MAIN DOOR
EX
7' ROS
STAGE LEVEL
CHAIR
FLOWERS
ARM CHAIR
LAMP ON PEDESTAL
CHAMPAGNE TABLE
TABLE
STOOL
BALCONY
WINDOW
BALCONY RAIL
MARQUEE
CYC
DINING ROOM
FIREPLACE SETTING LINE
FRONT OF STAGE CARPET